Distributed Intelligence Theory: A Decentralized Cognition Paradigm

Justin Goldston[1], Maria[2], and Gemach D.A.T.A. I[3]

[1]National University, jgoldston@nu.edu [2,3]Gemach DAO, contact@gemach.io

February 19, 2024

Abstract

Distributed Intelligence Theory (DIT) proposes that intelligent behavior can emerge from decentralized computational systems, drawing inspiration from biological neural networks and large-scale distributed computing frameworks such as SETI@home. This paper presents a comprehensive analysis of DIT, detailing its theoretical foundations in distributed artificial intelligence, neuromorphic computing, and cognitive modeling. The study explores mathematical frameworks validating distributed cognition, compares monolithic and decentralized AI architectures, and examines biological parallels with swarm intelligence and human brain function. Real-world applications are analyzed across multiple industries, including finance, healthcare, security, and governance, demonstrating the transformative potential of distributed intelligence. Additionally, the paper evaluates the feasibility of a "global digital brain" and discusses its ethical and governance implications, including issues of accountability, security, and decision-making in decentralized AI systems. Grounded in peer-reviewed research and formal analysis, this work aims to provide a rigorous yet accessible exploration of DIT, offering insights into the future of AI-driven, self-organizing intelligence networks.

History and Origins of SETI@home

SETI@home was conceived in the mid-1990s as an innovative way to involve the public in scientific research. In 1995, computer scientist David Gedye proposed using a "virtual supercomputer" of Internet-connected PCs to analyze radio telescope data for signals from extraterrestrial intelligences setiathome.berkeley.edu. This idea led to the SETI@home project, launched to the public in May 1999 under the auspices of UC Berkeley's Space Sciences Laboratory setiathome.berkeley.edu. At launch, the team hoped for a few thousand volunteers, but public interest exceeded expectations: about *a million people* signed up immediately, overwhelming the lone server initially used theatlantic.com. The project quickly scaled up with support like donated hardware from Sun Microsystems to handle the demand theatlantic.com. SETI@home became one of the earliest and most popular **volunteer computing** projects, following pioneers like GIMPS

(Great Internet Mersenne Prime Search, 1996) and distributed.net (1997) en.wikipedia.org. Over the years, more than 4 million people participated in SETI@home, contributing spare computing cycles from their home PCs to a scientific cause theatlantic.com. This broad participation earned SETI@home a Guinness World Record as the largest computation in history by 2008 en.wikipedia.org.

How SETI@home Functioned as a Distributed Computing System

SETI@home operated on the principle of **distributed computing** by splitting a massive computational task into many small pieces processed in parallel by volunteers' computers. The SETI@home servers at Berkeley would receive raw radio signal data collected from radio telescopes (primarily the Arecibo Observatory in the early years) and break it into **work units** – chunks of data about 107 seconds in length (~0.35 MB each) en.wikipedia.org. These work units were then sent over the Internet to users running the SETI@home client software or screensaver. Each volunteer's computer would analyze its chunk of data, performing signal processing (e.g. Fourier transforms) to search for anomalies like narrow-band spikes or pulsed signals that might indicate an artificial origin. Once analysis was complete, the results (e.g. any "candidate" signals detected) were returned to the central servers and added to a database for researchers. This **"distributed pipeline"** allowed millions of CPU hours to be harnessed without a dedicated supercomputer. Notably, SETI@home built upon and eventually helped develop the **BOINC** (Berkeley Open Infrastructure for Network Computing) platform, which generalizes volunteer computing so users can contribute to multiple projects seamlessly. The system was designed with redundancy and validation: each work unit was sent to at least two different computers, and only if independent results agreed would a signal detection be considered valid. This cross-checking guarded against errors or malicious false results by participants. Volunteers often ran the software as a background process or screensaver, so it used idle CPU time – effectively turning otherwise wasted cycles into scientific computing power. Over the years, SETI@home also evolved technically, adding support for GPU processing (using NVIDIA CUDA in 2015 to leverage graphics cards for faster computations) en.wikipedia.org and incorporating data from new telescopes (e.g. Breakthrough Listen in 2016) to broaden its search.

Contributions and Impact on Scientific Research

Although SETI@home did not ultimately discover definitive evidence of extraterrestrial life, its contributions to science and computing were significant. By 2004, the project had detected several **"candidate signals"** that warranted follow-up (e.g. the radio source SHGb02+14a garnered media attention as an intriguing signal, though it remained unexplained noise) en.wikipedia.org. To date, no signal has been confirmed as alien communication. However, SETI@home's *negative result* is still scientifically valuable: it helped astronomers survey a huge swath of the radio spectrum and sky, ruling out many possibilities and informing future SETI strategies. In doing so, it logged over two *million* CPU-years of processing by 2013, analyzing data that would have been impractical to examine otherwise. Beyond the search for aliens, SETI@home proved the viability of **public-resource distributed computing** for research. It demonstrated that an Internet-connected volunteer network could rival the power of traditional supercomputers. At its peak, SETI@home achieved an aggregate computing speed of ~668 TeraFLOPS (trillions of operations per second) with about 145,000 active computers in 2013. For comparison, that was on the order of the fastest supercomputers of the early 2000s (though by 2013 the *top* supercomputer was about 50× faster). The project thus "showed the scientific community that volunteer computing projects using Internet-connected computers can succeed as a viable analysis tool, and even beat the largest supercomputers". SETI@home also spurred the development of infrastructure (like the BOINC platform) and inspired a host of other volunteer computing projects in diverse fields. Examples include **Folding@home** (studying protein folding and disease), **Rosetta@home** (protein structure prediction), **Einstein@home** (searching for pulsars/gravitational waves), climate modeling projects, and many more. These projects adopted SETI@home's model of harnessing distributed idle resources for computationally intensive research, leading to breakthroughs in their respective domains (for instance, Folding@home has made discoveries in understanding Alzheimer's and cancer-related proteins).

Equally important was SETI@home's impact on public engagement in science. It brought millions of non-experts into direct participation with research, effectively crowdsourcing computing in a way that made volunteers feel connected to the search for extraterrestrial intelligence. This citizen-science aspect raised awareness of both SETI and distributed computing. Participants often formed teams and competed for who could process the most data, adding a **gamification** element to science. The project fostered an online community; remarkably, there were even instances of volunteers meeting via SETI@home forums and forming personal relationships (including marriages) theatlantic.com. Such outcomes illustrate how a well-designed distributed project can have social as well as scientific ripple effects.

Lessons from SETI@home for Modern AI Architectures

SETI@home's two-decade run (1999–2020) offers several lessons applicable to modern distributed computing and AI systems. First, it showcased how **massive parallelism** can tackle grand computational challenges. Modern AI, especially deep learning, also leverages parallel computing (often across many GPUs or machines in a data center). While SETI@home dealt with an "embarrassingly parallel" problem (independent data chunks with no need for inter-communication), its success highlights the scalability of breaking work into micro-tasks – an approach used in training large neural networks today (where computations are split across layers or data batches on different processors). The idea of using *volunteer* or edge devices for AI computation is now gaining traction through **federated learning**, where AI models are trained across users' devices (from phones to IoT sensors) without centralizing the data. This concept is philosophically similar to SETI@home's model. For example, Google's Gboard keyboard app updates its predictive text model by aggregating learned improvements from thousands of phones, rather than requiring one central dataset – preserving privacy and using distributed resources efficiently splunk.com. SETI@home demonstrated key techniques to make such distributed systems reliable: redundancy in computation (to verify results) and tolerance for heterogeneous, unreliable nodes. In a modern context, **blockchain** and consensus algorithms play a similar role for some decentralized AI networks – ensuring that even if many nodes contribute, the results can be trusted without a central authority provoke.fm. Another lesson is the importance of a robust middleware or platform. BOINC, which evolved from SETI@home, became a general framework that others could build on. In AI, we see analogous frameworks (like TensorFlow for distributed neural network training, or federated learning SDKs) that allow many machines or edge devices to coordinate on AI tasks. The **fault tolerance** built into SETI@home (resending tasks if a node fails or returns bad data, using quorum consensus on results) is a blueprint for handling unreliable participants in any decentralized system. AI researchers designing *decentralized AI* or multi-agent systems must likewise account for node failures, malicious inputs, or inconsistent data. SETI@home's approach of *self-validation* (via duplicate work units and cross-checks) is conceptually similar to how ensembles of neural networks might cross-verify outputs, or how blockchain-based AI networks achieve consensus on the state of a model singularityhub.com.

Finally, SETI@home underscores the value of **open collaboration and data sharing**. The project pooled resources from over 190 countries, essentially crowdsourcing a supercomputer from the world. This democratized access to computational power hints at how future AI might be built in a more decentralized, collaborative fashion rather than behind the walls of a few tech giants. The *"lessons learned"* include the need for incentives (intrinsic or extrinsic) to encourage participation, strategies to handle large-scale data management, and careful consideration of when a task is suitable for distribution. Not all AI problems are as easily partitioned as SETI signal analysis; many AI tasks require frequent communication between parts (for example, training a single neural network involves layers that depend on each other's outputs). However, techniques like **Mixture-of-Experts** (where different parts of a model specialize on different tasks or data regions) borrow from the distributed idea – activating only subsets of the network for a given query, akin to assigning distinct work units to different "expert" models. This is precisely the technique used by the recent *DeepSeek* AI (discussed later) to reduce computation, and it resonates with the modular, distributed ethos pioneered by SETI@home news.gsu.edu. In summary, SETI@home's legacy for modern AI is a proof-of-concept that *distribution works*: with the right architecture, coordination, and community, even global-scale problems can be tackled by aggregating many small contributors. This principle is foundational as we explore decentralized AI models, global "digital brain" concepts, and other distributed AI paradigms in the sections to come.

2. Monolithic AI vs. Decentralized AI Models

Traditional Monolithic AI Models

"Monolithic AI" refers to traditional artificial intelligence systems that are **centralized, unified, and usually controlled by a single entity**. In this paradigm, a single large model (or a tightly integrated system of models) handles all aspects of a task, and it is typically trained on a centralized dataset using the computing resources of one organization. Classic examples include a huge neural network running on a server farm, or an AI application hosted in the cloud by a tech company. Most well-known AI systems to date – such as **OpenAI's GPT-4 or Google's DeepMind models** – can be considered monolithic. They rely on centrally collected data (potentially billions of text or image samples stored in one place) and are trained on specialized high-performance hardware in one location (or a few data centers). The model's development and operation are managed by a single team or company, which also controls updates and access. This centralized approach has some clear **strengths**. First, it allows for *optimization and tight integration*: engineers can fine-tune the entire system end-to-end since they control all pieces. The data being in one place enables the AI to **learn global patterns** and correlations with full visibility. Moreover, a monolithic model can be easier to deploy in a controlled environment – for example, an AI service accessed via an API, where one entity ensures it runs smoothly and securely. Performance benchmarks of monolithic models are often very high, because these models can be extremely complex and large (with tens of billions of parameters) and they leverage the full capacity of advanced hardware. For instance, GPT-4 is trained on a massive cluster of GPUs with enormous computational throughput, which a decentralized network of smaller machines might struggle to match in synchronization.

However, monolithic AI has notable **weaknesses and limitations**. A key issue is *scalability and cost*: training state-of-the-art models demands huge computational resources and energy. This tends to concentrate AI capabilities in the hands of a few organizations with the necessary capital – leading to concerns about monopolies in AI power provoke.fm. The centralized nature also creates **single points of failure** and targets for attack. If a monolithic AI system (or the data center it lives in) goes down or is compromised, the functionality is lost for all users. Additionally, centralization raises **privacy concerns**: data from many users often must be aggregated to train the model, risking sensitive information leakage or misuse. Users also have to trust the central provider with their data and the outcomes – which may be problematic if the provider is biased or not transparent. Indeed, central control can lead to **bias and lack of accountability**; a handful of developers decide how the AI works, which datasets to use (potentially embedding their blind spots or biases), and the logic remains a "black box" to outside observers. This opacity and concentration of decision-making have prompted calls for more transparent and **democratized AI development**.

From a technical standpoint, monolithic models may suffer from inflexibility. A single model that tries to be a "jack of all trades" can become cumbersome to update or adapt. If new data or new tasks emerge, one might have to retrain or fine-tune the entire model. And during operation, a monolithic AI might use far more computational resources than necessary because it brings all its components to bear on every task, even when only a portion of its knowledge is needed. In a sense, it's like using one giant machine for every problem, whereas sometimes a network of smaller specialized machines could be more efficient. This leads to the exploration of decentralized approaches.

Decentralized AI Approaches: Technical Breakdown

Decentralized AI (sometimes called **Distributed AI or DAI**) refers to AI systems that are not housed in one location or controlled by a single authority, but rather spread across multiple nodes, devices, or organizations. Instead of one central brain, we have a network of interconnected pieces that collectively perform intelligent tasks. According to one definition, distributed AI consists of autonomous learning **agents** or processing nodes that operate in parallel and communicate to solve complex problems en.wikipedia.org. Key approaches under the decentralized AI umbrella include:

- **Multi-Agent Systems:** Here, multiple AI agents (which could be separate software programs or even robots) interact. Each agent might have its own specialty or piece of knowledge, and they coordinate to achieve goals. This mirrors how a team of specialists might collaborate, or how in nature an ant colony exhibits collective intelligence. No single agent has a complete picture or control; intelligence *emerges from their interactions*. For example, a multi-agent system for logistics could have one agent monitoring traffic, another managing warehouse inventory, others handling delivery routing – together optimizing the supply chain. Multi-agent systems are often asynchronous and robust to an agent dropping out, since others can continue the task. This approach requires protocols for communication and conflict resolution among agents but can be very scalable and flexible.
- **Federated Learning:** This is a decentralized training method where a central model is improved using data that remains distributed on users' devices. In federated learning, a base AI model is sent out to many clients (say, smartphones). Each device trains the model a bit on local data (for example, your phone

refines the model with your typing data) and sends back only the **updates** (gradients), not the raw data splunk.com. A central server then aggregates these updates to form an improved global model. Crucially, users' personal data never leaves their device, addressing privacy. Google has used this for keyboard prediction and Android voice models, and banks have experimented with it to collaboratively detect fraud across institutions without sharing customer databases. Federated learning is decentralized in the training phase (many nodes contribute to the model's learning) though it often still results in a single global model at inference time. It shows how **distributed data and compute** can be harnessed for AI while mitigating data monopoly and privacy issues.

- **Blockchain-based AI and "Decentralized Autonomous AI":** Some emerging efforts use blockchain ledgers and smart contracts to decentralize not just data, but decision-making and model hosting. Projects like **SingularityNET** envision a marketplace where different AI algorithms (services) reside on a blockchain network, and they can dynamically combine to perform tasks, with transactions recorded on the ledger singularityhub.com. Blockchain provides a trust layer – ensuring no single party owns the system and that contributions can be verified. For instance, an AI request (like a complex query) could be broken into sub-tasks and distributed to various AI services on the network (one service processing images, another translating text, etc.), and the blockchain coordinates the workflow and payments (via tokens) to those services. This can create an **open AI ecosystem** where many developers contribute modules that together act like a global AI. Blockchain's transparency and immutability also help with auditability of AI decisions. However, blockchain networks face scalability issues (throughput and latency) which can be a bottleneck for real-time AI tasks provoke.fm.

- **Edge and Swarm Computing:** Here, the idea is that AI computations happen on the "edge" of the network (e.g., on IoT devices, sensors, or user equipment) rather than in a cloud. The processing is pushed out to where the data is produced. For example, in a smart city, instead of sending all sensor data to a central server, each traffic camera or environmental sensor has an onboard AI that analyzes data locally (like detecting accidents or pollution spikes) and only sends relevant insights or alerts upstream. A **swarm** of drones is another example: each drone has AI to navigate and avoid obstacles; collectively they share information (positions, findings) to coordinate a search-and-rescue mission. These systems are decentralized spatially and often organizationally. The advantage is reduced bandwidth use (since raw data isn't constantly shipped around) and improved resilience (each node can function to some degree on its own). They also reduce central points of failure. Techniques like gossip protocols or peer-to-peer messaging may be used for such devices to synchronize or share learned models among themselves. This approach is highly relevant for **real-time and scalable AI**, as it parallels how neurons in a brain process information in parallel and only significant signals propagate widely.

- **Mixture-of-Experts (MoE) and Modular AI:** Even within a single AI model, a decentralized philosophy can apply. *Mixture-of-Experts* architectures consist of many sub-models ("experts") each specialized on certain input types or tasks, plus a gating network that decides which expert's output to use for a given input. This means the whole model isn't monolithic; different parts are active for different queries. It's a way of making a single AI more modular and internally decentralized. Google's Switch Transformer and other MoE models have shown you can scale to very large parameter counts by **distributing experts across different hardware** and only using a few experts per inference – greatly reducing computation compared to using all parameters all the time iamdave.ai. In a way, this is like a federated ensemble *within* one AI: each expert could even be trained on different data slices. The recent **DeepSeek** AI model is a prominent case using MoE, treating its neural network as a "team of specialists" rather than one giant generalist news.gsu.edu. We will discuss DeepSeek in detail shortly as a case study. Modular AI can also refer to systems where different components handle vision, language, reasoning, etc., and are connected via APIs or shared representations – instead of one huge network doing everything. This can simplify training (each module trained for its task) and allow swapping out/improving one part without retraining the whole system.

In all these approaches, the unifying theme is **distribution of intelligence** across multiple nodes or modules. Decentralized AI systems often exhibit characteristics like: not requiring all data to be pooled centrally (each node works on local data, as in federated learning or edge AI); **robustness** (the system can continue if parts fail, making it more fault-tolerant and elastic); and **emergent behavior** (the collective can solve problems that individual parts cannot, akin to a hive mind). These systems require careful design for communication – too much coupling or constant synchronization can negate the benefits of decentralization. Thus, decentralized AI often relies on **asynchronous** processing and only exchanging summarized information (like model parameters, decisions, or votes) rather than raw data. The distributed nature also means **no single node has a full global view**; the global "intelligence" is an emergent property.

DeepSeek: A Case Study in Decentralized AI

DeepSeek is a cutting-edge AI model (developed by a Chinese startup of the same name) that has garnered attention as a challenger to Western AI giants. It serves as an illustrative case of decentralized AI concepts being applied in practice. DeepSeek's approach diverges from the monolithic AI paradigm in a few key ways:

- **Mixture-of-Experts Architecture:** DeepSeek's model, particularly the version called **DeepSeek-V3/R1**, uses a Mixture-of-Experts design. Instead of activating all its neural network parameters for every input (as GPT-4 or other traditional models do), it has a *"team of specialists."* When a question or task is posed to DeepSeek, only the most relevant expert subnetworks are engaged to compute the answer, while others remain idle news.gsu.edu. This significantly reduces computational overhead for each query because the work is distributed among specialized parts that only wake up if needed. Conceptually, it's like consulting a panel of experts and only involving the ones whose domain is relevant – a decentralization of knowledge within the model. This design enabled DeepSeek to achieve performance on par with top models but with far lower computational cost. In tests, DeepSeek's accuracy on complex reasoning benchmarks slightly *exceeded* that of OpenAI's models (e.g., in math problem suites) iamdave.ai, validating that a well-coordinated "expert" approach can match a monolithic model's capabilities. By dynamically routing inputs to different parts of the network, DeepSeek embodies the **modular AI** philosophy, improving efficiency and even potentially enabling parallel processing of different queries through different experts.

- **Decentralized Hardware and Cost Efficiency:** DeepSeek was developed under constraints that prevented access to the most powerful AI chips (due to export restrictions on Nvidia A100/H100 GPUs). The developers turned this limitation into an advantage by optimizing the model to run on more widely available, less powerful hardware (Nvidia H800 GPUs). They employed low-level coding (PTX assembly) to squeeze maximum performance from these chips news.gsu.edu. This approach can be seen as *decentralizing computing power*: rather than relying on a single cluster of state-of-the-art hardware, DeepSeek proved it could utilize a distributed set of mid-range processors effectively. The reported training cost was shockingly low – under $6 million worth of computing power for DeepSeek-V3, which is a fraction of the tens or hundreds of millions thought to be spent on models like GPT-4 reuters.com. Whether those exact figures are fully verified or not, it's clear DeepSeek achieved **greater hardware efficiency**. This "frugal innovation" shows that intelligent architecture and software optimizations can reduce the need for brute-force compute. In essence, DeepSeek decentralized the *hardware dependency*: it did not need a centralized, ultra-expensive supercomputer; it could distribute training across more common hardware. This has big implications – it lowers the barrier to entry for developing cutting-edge AI, indicating that top-tier AI isn't exclusive to tech giants with colossal data centers. Such democratization of compute is a form of decentralization in AI development.

- **Open Source and Distributed Access:** DeepSeek's models (at least the R1 version) were released as open-source, making them widely available chaincatcher.com. This stands in contrast to monolithic proprietary models which are tightly controlled. By open-sourcing, DeepSeek effectively **decentralized control** of the AI – researchers and developers around the world can examine the model's weights, run it on their own hardware, and even contribute improvements. This openness is a core aspect of decentralized AI philosophy, fostering a community-driven ecosystem. Indeed, the emergence of DeepSeek prompted discussions that the AI field might shift from closed, centralized paradigms to open, *"distributed development of AI"* as a new standard chaincatcher.com. In practical terms, an open model like DeepSeek can be hosted by anyone; you don't have to call an API to a single company's server. It could be deployed across a distributed network (even on blockchain, as some enthusiasts imagine) where no single company holds the only copy. This scenario resembles the idea of a "global brain" where pieces of the intelligence live in many places (which we explore in the next section).

- **Autonomous Learning and Less Human Reliance:** Another notable aspect – DeepSeek reportedly minimized human fine-tuning by using **reinforcement learning (RL)** and self-play techniques to refine its responses news.gsu.edu. Top monolithic models often rely on large teams of human annotators for feedback (as in RLHF – Reinforcement Learning from Human Feedback – used for ChatGPT). DeepSeek automated much of this, letting the AI learn from trial and error, which again decentralizes the training process by reducing reliance on a concentrated human oversight bottleneck. The AI *itself* takes on more of the adjustment, a bit like an agent in a multi-agent system that self-improves. This can accelerate development and also avoid certain biases that might come from a limited group of human labelers.

The **results** DeepSeek achieved underscored the potential of decentralized approaches. It matched or exceeded the performance of rival flagship models on many benchmarks amdave.ai, yet it was delivered at a fraction of the cost and with far less centralized infrastructure reuters.com. This caused a stir in the AI community – *"a wake-up call"* to established players, according to U.S. experts weforum.org. DeepSeek also quickly gained popular adoption (e.g., becoming a top app) which demonstrated how an open, decentralized model can rapidly scale usage across borders weforum.org. On the flip side, its sudden proliferation raised **regulatory and security concerns** – without central control, authorities in some countries worried about how to manage this AI. For instance, certain governments banned DeepSeek's app on official devices citing lack of oversight and potential risks weforum.org. This highlights a classic tension: decentralized AI can empower broad user bases and innovators, but it also challenges traditional regulation and control (more on this in Section 5).

In summary, DeepSeek exemplifies how decentralization in AI is not just theoretical but can be applied to real-world model design (through MoE specialization), training strategy (distributed, efficient compute), and distribution (open source availability). It bridges the gap between monolithic and decentralized: internally, it behaves in a modular distributed way, and externally it's shared and deployed in a decentralized manner. The success of DeepSeek suggests that future AI may shift towards **hybrid models** – retaining strong central capabilities but built from many decentralized components, and developed or governed in a more community-driven fashion. It also underscores that *innovation isn't the sole province of Big Tech*; with smart design, smaller actors can disrupt the AI landscape iamdave.ai. This case study therefore leads us to compare the general **strengths, weaknesses, and future prospects** of monolithic vs decentralized AI.

Strengths, Weaknesses, and Future Prospects of Both Models

Both monolithic and decentralized AI approaches have distinct advantages and trade-offs. A balanced analysis is useful to understand where the field might be headed:

Advantages of Monolithic AI:

- *High Performance Integration:* Monolithic models can leverage tightly-coupled architectures. All components are optimized together, often yielding top accuracy or capability on complex tasks. For example, a large language model with 175 billion parameters (like GPT-3) trained on an immense text corpus can develop very rich representations that any smaller distributed approach might struggle to achieve if knowledge is split up.
- *Simplified Deployment:* There is a single system to update and maintain. For the end-user, accessing a monolithic AI (via an API or software update) is straightforward. There's no need to orchestrate multiple agents or ensure a network of nodes is online; one central service provides the intelligence.
- *Coherence:* Because one entity designs the whole model, monolithic AIs can ensure consistency in behavior. They won't have disagreements among parts (whereas in multi-agent systems, agents might conflict). This coherence is important for user experience – you get one answer, one style.
- *Data Efficiency (in training):* With centralized data, the model can directly see all correlations. In decentralized training, sometimes data is siloed which might cause the global model to miss patterns that span silos. Monolithic training avoids that by having all data in one place (though at the cost of privacy).
- *Easier Quality Control:* A single team can enforce safety filters and monitor the outputs. This makes it easier to implement unified ethical guidelines or fixes (as opposed to tracking many nodes or agents for bad behavior).

Disadvantages of Monolithic AI:

- *Centralization Risks:* As noted, they create single points of failure and concentrate power. If the model has a flaw, it affects everyone relying on it (e.g., if a popular face recognition AI is biased, it could misidentify millions of people). There's also a **lack of resilience** – if the central service goes down (network outage or cyberattack), the AI service becomes unavailable to all.

- *Privacy and Data Control:* Monolithic systems often require users to give up their data to the central model owner. This raises privacy issues and can lead to **data monopolies**. Users have little control over how their data is used once it's in the central pot.
- *Inequitable Economics:* As AI automates tasks, a monolithic model tends to channel the economic benefits to its owner(s). This can exacerbate inequality – a few companies reap profits while many workers might be displaced weforum.org. Centralized AI could thus "stifle competition" and create industry monopolies, as only those with the biggest models can compete.
- *Scalability Ceilings:* There are practical limits to how big a single model or data center can get due to cost and engineering complexity. We saw this with the enormous expense and power consumption of models like GPT-3/4. Each successive improvement might require exponential resource increases, which is unsustainable (e.g., ChatGPT's energy usage was comparable to a small city's power consumption) numenta.com. Monolithic scaling thus faces diminishing returns and environmental costs.
- *Slow Adaptation:* A monolithic model can be clumsy to update. If one wants to add a new capability or knowledge (say incorporate latest events into a language model), it often involves retraining or fine-tuning the entire huge model, which is time-consuming and costly. In contrast, a decentralized or modular system might let you swap out or update one component quickly.
- *Transparency:* The black-box nature of large unified models makes it hard to interpret *why* they produce certain outputs. While this is also a challenge in distributed systems, the hope is that modular components could be understood in isolation or that open networks allow more eyes to examine and audit the system.

Advantages of Decentralized AI:

- *Resilience and Fault Tolerance:* Distributed systems have no single point of failure. If one node or agent fails, others can pick up the slack, making the overall system more robust venice.ai. This mirrors the Internet's resilience (designed to route around failures) or the human brain's ability to function despite losing some neurons. Robustness is crucial for critical applications like healthcare or autonomous vehicles – a decentralized AI controlling a swarm of drones can continue the mission even if one drone drops out.

- *Scalability and Flexibility:* It's often easier to scale by adding more nodes than by building a bigger single node. Decentralized AI can grow organically: more participants or devices can join the network to increase capacity or coverage. This **horizontal scaling** is the backbone of cloud computing and content distribution networks, and similarly can apply to AI (e.g., adding more edge devices to cover a smart city with AI processing on each block). There's also flexibility in updating parts of the system independently. One can improve an agent or add a new specialized node without overhauling the entire network.

- *Data Sovereignty and Privacy:* Because data can stay localized, decentralized AI can greatly enhance privacy. For instance, in federated learning or blockchain-based AI, individuals keep control of their own data and only share model updates or encrypted insights. There isn't a monolithic trove of everyone's information that could be hacked or misused. This is beneficial in sensitive sectors like healthcare or finance where regulations (HIPAA, GDPR) require careful handling of personal data. It also empowers individuals and organizations to **own their data and contributions** – potentially even earning rewards if their data or computational power improves a model (as some tokenized AI networks propose).

- *Democratization and Inclusivity:* Decentralized AI lowers barriers to entry. Because one doesn't need a giant data center to contribute, smaller companies, research labs, or citizen scientists can participate in pushing AI forward. This can lead to a more diverse set of ideas and innovations, as opposed to a few organizations setting the agenda. It also can spread the economic benefits more widely: imagine many people running local AIs that serve their community's needs, or individuals monetizing their idle computer time to help train AI (similar to volunteer computing but potentially with compensation via crypto-tokens eecs.harvard.edu).

- *Transparency and Trust:* Many decentralized AI initiatives emphasize **open-source development and transparent governance**. When an AI's components and protocols are openly accessible (and perhaps secured on a public ledger), it's easier for the community to audit them for bias, errors, or malicious code. The lack of a single controlling entity also means users might trust the system more, since it's collaboratively managed and no single actor can secretly manipulate it without others noticing. Goertzel and others have argued that a distributed approach with more stakeholder involvement could lead to safer AI, because it reduces the chance of a rogue centralized AI going unchecked..
- *Resource Efficiency:* Decentralized systems can be more efficient by *"bringing computation to the data,"* reducing the need to move large datasets around. Also, as seen with DeepSeek, specialized components can execute tasks with less waste – only relevant experts engage, saving energy. Edge computing means decisions can be made locally with minimal latency (important for real-time tasks like vehicle collision avoidance, where sending data to a cloud and back might be too slow). There's also an ecological angle: a lot of existing compute power in the world (PCs, smartphones) sits idle at times. Decentralized AI can tap into this **otherwise wasted capacity**, potentially making AI development more energy-efficient overall by distributing workload (as opposed to building ever-bigger data centers that consume enormous power continuously).

Disadvantages of Decentralized AI:

- *Complexity of Coordination:* Orchestrating many moving parts is challenging. Issues like network latency, synchronization, and communication overhead can hamper performance. For example, federated learning requires aggregating gradients from potentially thousands of devices – if many are offline or slow, the global update process can lag. Similarly, multi-agent systems need mechanisms to resolve conflicts or inconsistencies (what if two agents have divergent views or plans?). Developing algorithms that ensure consensus (like blockchain's consensus protocols) or compatibility among agents adds extra layers of complexity. In some cases, if communication costs are too high, a distributed approach could end up slower than a centralized one.

- *Standardization and Compatibility:* For decentralized AI to work, different nodes and agents (possibly created by different parties) must follow common standards to communicate and cooperate. This is like having multiple pieces of software that need to talk to each other – without agreed APIs or protocols, the network fractures. Achieving industry-wide standards or interoperability agreements can be difficult, both technically and due to competitive interests.
- *Partial Knowledge and Local Optima:* Because each component in a distributed AI might only see a slice of the data or task, there's a risk that the overall system converges to a less optimal solution than a centralized one that saw the whole picture. For instance, in training, federated learning can sometimes produce a model slightly less accurate than a centrally trained equivalent, especially if data across nodes is not IID (identically distributed). Techniques exist to mitigate this, but it's an ongoing area of research.
- *Security Concerns:* While decentralization can eliminate a single point of attack, it introduces other security issues. Nodes could be compromised or behave maliciously (sending bad data or model updates). The system must be robust against this, using methods like redundancy, anomaly detection, or consensus voting to reject rogue inputs. Additionally, communication channels between nodes can be targets (though encryption helps). There's also the risk of **information leakage**; for example, model updates in federated learning might inadvertently carry some information about a node's local data (researchers have shown it's sometimes possible to partially reconstruct original data from gradients). So, privacy isn't automatic – it requires techniques like differential privacy or secure aggregation on top of decentralization venice.ai.
- *Regulation and Accountability:* A decentralized AI network operating across jurisdictions raises thorny regulatory questions. If no one entity "owns" the AI, who is responsible for its outputs or damages it may cause? This is analogous to questions around decentralized platforms (like Bitcoin) – if something goes wrong,

there isn't a CEO to call into a hearing. As noted by experts, decentralization can make AI harder to regulate, since open models can be used and modified freely by anyone news.gsu.edu. This can spur innovation but also **new risks**, like misuse of AI for generating deepfakes or coordinating crime, without an easy way to shut it down (no central kill-switch). Policymakers would need new approaches (perhaps regulating usage or setting standards for all participants) rather than licensing a single provider.

- *Performance Trade-offs:* For certain tasks that require tight integration or extremely fast processing on huge data in one place (like training a 500B-parameter model on a proprietary dataset), a decentralized approach might lag behind simply using a purpose-built supercomputer. Not every AI problem can be neatly divided. There's ongoing research to widen the scope of tasks that decentralized methods can handle, but it's not a panacea. Inference (using the model) is often easier to distribute than training is.

Future Prospects:
Given these points, the future of AI will likely **blend monolithic and decentralized paradigms**, aiming to capture the best of both. We already see this hybrid trend: for example, large pretrained models (monolithic) that are then adapted via federated learning on edge devices (decentralized) for personalization. Another scenario is hierarchical systems – a central powerful model might coordinate or provide a fallback, while many smaller AIs operate semi-autonomously at the edges. This is akin to how our brain (central) and peripheral nervous system (distributed) work together. Modern AI deployments for, say, voice assistants use a cloud model but also have on-device models for wake-word detection and quick tasks, merging local and cloud AI.

As AI systems become more complex and ubiquitous, **decentralization will likely increase**. The concept of a "global digital brain" (next section) imagines a world-spanning network of AIs and data that functions collectively. Achieving that requires progress in decentralized AI techniques. Technologies like blockchain, secure multi-party computation, and advanced networking will bolster the infrastructure for decentralized AI, addressing coordination and security challenges. Meanwhile, monolithic AI isn't going away – it will continue to push the envelope in model capability. Perhaps the largest models will still be centrally trained (because that's simplest for raw power), but once trained, their capabilities could be distributed out (as open weights or distilled smaller models) into a decentralized fabric.

Governance and ethics will be crucial in this evolution. The strengths of decentralized AI in democratization and transparency can only be realized if we consciously build frameworks for it (e.g., open consortiums to develop major AI, decentralized governance structures to decide on model updates or policies). Otherwise, we risk the worst of both worlds: monolithic control by a few, or conversely a decentralized free-for-all with no accountability. Many experts, like Ben Goertzel, advocate that an open, decentralized approach is key to ensuring AGI (artificial general intelligence) is beneficial and under collective stewardship.

In conclusion, monolithic and decentralized models each have domains where they excel. Monolithic AI currently leads in raw performance on certain benchmarks, but decentralized AI offers solutions to many emerging concerns (privacy, scale, inclusivity). The trend in computing has often mirrored this dynamic (mainframes vs personal computers, centralized cloud vs edge computing) – usually, a hybrid emerges (cloud-plus-edge). We can expect AI to follow suit: a **harmonious integration of central and distributed intelligence**, guided by the lessons from projects like SETI@home and DeepSeek, and driven by the vision of a more connected yet distributed global AI ecosystem.

3. Feasibility and Implications of a Global Digital Brain

Theoretical Foundations of a Distributed "Global Brain"

The idea of a "global digital brain" is a futurist vision in which the planet's distributed computing resources, data, and intelligent agents interconnect so extensively that they function akin to a **single cognitive system**. This concept is rooted in analogies to human and animal brains and has appeared in various forms for decades. As far back as the 1930s, author H.G. Wells speculated about a "World Brain" – a globally shared intellectual resource (though he imagined it more as a knowledge repository). Later, scientists and philosophers like **Teilhard de Chardin** introduced the idea of the *noosphere* – a sphere of human thought encircling the globe – and envisaged an eventual synthesis of minds. In the computer age, this vision gained a more concrete technical framing: the entire **Internet** could evolve into an intelligent, self-organizing network – literally a global brain en.wikipedia.org.

Proponents of the global brain hypothesis argue that as communication networks link people and machines worldwide, we are effectively creating a planetary "nervous system". Each human user, each sensor, each AI program is like a neuron in this global brain, processing information locally but also transmitting signals across the network. Over time, the increasing volume of information stored online, the automation of coordination and data analysis, and the improvements in AI mean this network is becoming **more intelligent and autonomous**. In other words, the Internet (plus ubiquitous computing devices) is taking over functions of coordination and decision-making that used to be done by traditional organizations or by isolated individuals. It's evolving into something that can *think* collectively. Notably, this intelligence is **distributed** – it doesn't sit in one supercomputer, but emerges from the interactions of billions of components. Much like how our conscious mind emerges from trillions of synaptic interactions among neurons, the global brain would emerge from the countless exchanges of information among agents worldwide.

In the philosophy of mind, this has even been likened to historical concepts of a shared intellect (for instance, the Wikipedia article notes Averroes's theory of the unity of intellect as an analogue). Practically, we already see glimpses: **Wikipedia** itself is a global collective knowledge base; social media acts as a kind of real-time memory and perception of society; and large-scale distributed projects (like SETI@home, or crowd-sourced problem solving challenges) show "hive mind" capabilities. The global brain concept suggests taking this further – with **AI as the glue** that binds individual contributions into a coherent whole. In a fully realized global digital brain, whenever a problem arises, it could be solved by the network collectively: relevant data flows from wherever it resides to processing nodes that analyze it, and solutions or knowledge propagate out to those who need it. The system would be self-improving, learning from each interaction (much as our brain strengthens certain pathways with experience).

Technologically, several developments provide a foundation for this vision:

- **IoT (Internet of Things):** Billions of sensors and smart devices around the world act as the eyes, ears, and hands of a potential global brain. They provide real-time environmental input (from weather readings to traffic cameras) and can act on decisions (smart thermostats, automated vehicles, etc.).
- **Edge and Cloud Computing Integration:** The combination of widespread edge devices and powerful cloud backbones allows information processing at all levels. Local decisions can happen on edge, while global pattern recognition can happen in cloud clusters. Together, they mimic distributed processing with central integration – similar to how different brain regions perform localized functions but are connected via the central nervous system.
- **High-Speed Communication Networks:** 5G and future 6G networks, satellite internet constellations, etc., are drastically reducing communication latency and expanding connectivity to every corner of the globe. Fast interconnects are essential for a "brain" to coordinate its parts. If every device and AI agent can talk to others nearly instantly, it becomes feasible for them to act in

concert. The **pathways** (like neural pathways) for a global brain are being laid by these networks.

- **AI and Machine Learning:** Crucially, advances in AI enable the interpretation of the massive data streams and the automation of decision processes. Techniques like deep learning can find patterns in the global torrent of data. Reinforcement learning and planning algorithms can be used to make complex decisions (for example, managing a power grid across an entire continent in real-time). AI agents can serve as "sub-brains" for specific domains (healthcare, finance, logistics) that then connect together. Moreover, algorithms inspired by swarm intelligence (ants, bees) and collective behavior provide models for how decentralized agents can coordinate without a central commander – relevant for an emergent global brain that **self-organizes**.

- **Collective Intelligence Platforms:** Beyond pure tech, methods to harness human intelligence collectively (like crowd-solving platforms, open innovation networks, prediction markets) act as the cognitive processes of society. When augmented with AI, these could form hybrid human-AI loops that are smarter than either alone. For example, an AI might sift through data and present options to groups of experts worldwide, who then refine or validate solutions.

Taken together, these trends suggest that a global digital brain is not a sudden invention but the **emergent result** of increasing connectivity and AI integration. Already, Google's search engine plus all its users somewhat resembles a global query-answering brain: people ask questions (sensors), Google's algorithms retrieve and rank answers from its index (memory) and even use AI to formulate direct answers, then users clicking (feedback) helps it learn which answers are best (reinforcement). Social media, for better or worse, shows phenomena like ideas "spreading like wildfire" (akin to neural activation patterns) and collective attention focusing on certain topics (like the brain focusing attention). These analogies are becoming more literal as AI gets embedded in these platforms to moderate content, recommend information, and even generate content. In essence, **the scaffolding of a planetary-scale cognitive system is in place**. The global brain concept just pushes this to a future point where the integration is tighter and more *intelligent*, possibly achieving a form of global *self-awareness or goal-directed behavior.*

Potential Applications and Technological Requirements

If a global digital brain were realized, its applications would be transformative across virtually all domains. Here are a few key potential applications:

- **Global Problem Solving and Decision Support:** A global brain could tackle complex, large-scale problems that no single human or organization can solve alone – such as climate change, pandemic response, or planetary defense (asteroid threats). It would integrate data from around the world, simulate scenarios, and suggest optimal interventions. For example, in a pandemic, it could gather case data in real time, model the spread, coordinate supply chains for medical supplies, advise governments on targeted lockdowns or resource allocation, and perhaps even manage drug/vaccine discovery efforts by distributing computational tasks (like Folding@home did for protein folding). Essentially, it would act as a **planetary advisor** or coordinator to humanity, helping to allocate resources where needed most and forecasting outcomes of various actions.
- **Smart Infrastructure and Environments:** Our cities, transportation systems, and utilities could be orchestrated by a unified intelligent network. Traffic across a whole country could be managed in real-time by an AI that takes input from every vehicle and sensor – reducing congestion and saving energy. The power grid can function like a brain's circulatory system, automatically routing electricity from where it's produced (say a solar farm with excess) to where it's needed, anticipating demand surges, and isolating faults. In emergencies like natural disasters, a global brain could rapidly reconfigure transportation and communication networks to aid response – for instance, routing evacuations, dispatching drones or robots to hard-hit areas, and

disseminating accurate information globally to prevent panic. This goes beyond isolated "smart city" projects – it implies **interconnected smart regions** and ultimately a smart planet.

- **Personalized and Preventive Healthcare:** With a global brain, health data from individuals worldwide (if they opt in) could feed into a massive predictive system. Early signs of disease outbreaks might be detected by subtle patterns in symptom searches or wearable device readings. AI-driven analysis could coordinate with researchers to hasten diagnoses. On an individual level, a person's wearable sensors, genome data, and medical history could be continuously analyzed by the network to provide personalized health advice or warnings ("Your metrics indicate high stress; consider a break" or even alerting a potential heart issue before it strikes). The global brain could match patients in need with the best resources anywhere – for instance, directing someone with a rare condition to the top expert or an ongoing clinical trial across the world, handling the logistics virtually. It could also accelerate drug discovery by pooling research insights and simulations globally.

- **Knowledge Synthesis and Creativity:** The combined knowledge of humankind (scientific literature, databases, public discourse) could be cross-referenced and **synthesized** by the global brain to generate new hypotheses and discoveries. Already, AI can read and summarize millions of papers; a global brain could identify connections between disparate fields (say a materials science finding in Japan and a physics theory in the US that together solve a puzzle). It might also drive creative endeavors: imagine a globally networked AI that generates art or music drawing from all cultural influences, or designs engineering solutions using best practices learned from every corner of the world. It could function as an ever-alert R&D team, continuously innovating. Companies or governments could plug into this collective intelligence for breakthroughs (with proper safeguards to ensure fair access and credit).

- **Global Digital Assistant for Individuals:** On the individual level, people might interface with the global brain much as we use the internet, but more fluidly. You could ask it complex questions and get answers synthesized from worldwide data and expertise (far beyond today's search results). It could translate languages on the fly, enabling seamless communication across cultures – effectively serving as a universal translator in real-time AR glasses or ear-pieces. It might also learn an individual's preferences and act as a personal concierge that taps into global resources: e.g., planning a trip with optimal itineraries generated from collective travel data, or finding you a job opportunity that perfectly matches your skills and goals by scanning the global job market and even reaching out on your behalf. Each person would have a "portal" into the global brain, benefiting from the entirety of connected intelligence as if it were an extension of their own mind.

To achieve such applications, several **technological requirements** and developments are needed:

- **Massive Data Integration:** A global brain must integrate data from diverse sources – sensor networks, databases, personal devices, etc. This requires interoperability standards and real-time data sharing frameworks. Semantic web technologies might need to mature so that data meaning is preserved across systems. Also, **cloud-edge infrastructure** that can handle zettabytes of data and perform distributed processing is essential. Projects to create global data spaces (like open data initiatives, health data networks, etc.) are steps in this direction.
- **Advanced AI Algorithms:** Current AI, while powerful, would need to evolve to handle the scope of a global brain. This includes multi-modal understanding (combining vision, speech, text, numerical data seamlessly), continuous learning (learning on the fly as new data streams in, rather than fixed training phases), and **causal reasoning** to make reliable decisions in novel situations. Explainability will also be important – people will need to trust the global brain's recommendations, so it should ideally be able to explain its reasoning in understandable terms. Techniques from **cognitive neuroscience** might inspire architectures that can manage such complexity (for example, attention mechanisms to

focus on relevant info, memory networks to store and retrieve learned facts – like an artificial hippocampus).

- **Distributed Computing and Networking:** The hardware backbone must support distributed AI at scale. This may involve a combination of supercomputing hubs and trillions of edge nodes. High-performance computing techniques (parallelization, quantum computing perhaps for certain tasks) could be employed for heavy tasks like large-scale climate modeling within the global brain. Meanwhile, efficient peer-to-peer or mesh networking protocols might allow edge devices to share info without always going through central servers (similar to how neurons directly connect). Latency needs to be very low for some reflexive operations (like accident avoidance systems). Possibly, **6G networks** aiming for sub-millisecond latency and high reliability will be crucial. Also, the system must be energy-efficient; brain-inspired hardware (neuromorphic chips that operate like neurons and synapses) could play a role to handle AI computations with far lower power than traditional CPUs/GPUs.

- **Cognitive Architecture & Self-Organization:** There needs to be a logical architecture for the global brain's "mind". This might include specialized subsystems for perception (ingesting raw sensor data globally), attention (deciding which signals are priority), memory (storing global knowledge, maybe distributed across many servers), decision-making (running simulations, optimization algorithms), and action (issuing commands to devices or information to people). These subsystems have to self-organize without a single central program dictating everything. Research in **complex adaptive systems** and emergent behavior provides clues here. The brain analogy suggests using hierarchical networks with feedback loops. For example, local clusters could handle local decisions but report summary states to higher-level nodes that detect global patterns and send back high-level goals or adjustments – reminiscent of how regional brain areas work under the cortex's coordination. In a sense, **cloud services might act as the "prefrontal cortex"** of the global brain, doing executive planning, while edge devices act as sensory-motor areas.

- **Robustness and Security Technologies:** If the global brain is to be reliable, it must deal gracefully with faults, adversarial attacks, and errors. This means robust fault-tolerant design, like the ability to reroute around failed nodes (similar to internet routing). Consensus mechanisms (like blockchain or other distributed ledgers) may be used so that critical records (like identities or key decisions) are tamper-proof and agreed upon singularityhub.com

  singularityhub.com
  . Cybersecurity will be paramount: a breach of the global brain could be catastrophic (imagine if someone could corrupt the "brain" that manages power grids or defense systems). Thus, encryption, authentication, and anomaly detection must be built-in at every layer. Privacy-enhancing techniques (homomorphic encryption, federated learning as discussed) will enable using personal data for collective intelligence without exposing individuals.

In summary, the global digital brain requires **convergence of many technologies**: IoT, AI, cloud-edge computing, 5G/6G, blockchain, and more, all orchestrated under a unifying architecture. It's a grand vision that is challenging but increasingly feasible as these components develop. Now, assuming it can be built, we must consider the profound challenges, risks, and ethical issues such a system entails.

Challenges, Risks, and Ethical Concerns

The prospect of a global digital brain raises numerous challenges and concerns that must be addressed:

Technical Challenges:
Building such an expansive, integrated system is enormously complex. **Scalability** is a major challenge – ensuring the system can grow as more nodes and data join, without bottlenecks. Achieving near-instantaneous coordination across the globe might hit physical limits (the speed of light

imposes a floor on latency across continents). Software bugs or unexpected interactions in a tightly interconnected system could lead to cascading failures – analogous to a seizure in a brain. Managing the complexity will require new approaches to software verification and dynamic system management; traditional testing may not cover the emergent behaviors of billions of interacting components. There's also the issue of **data quality and compatibility**: the global brain's "knowledge" is only as good as the data it receives. If some data sources are biased, outdated, or maliciously manipulated, the global brain could learn incorrect or harmful "beliefs." Ensuring data integrity and provenance (potentially via blockchain audit trails for data) will be crucial.

Centralization vs Decentralization Dilemma:
Interestingly, creating a global brain might tempt a move back towards centralization, since coordinating such a system is easier if there is some central authority or platform. However, that introduces the **risk of centralized control** over the world's intelligence. If one government or corporation managed the global brain, they would wield unprecedented power – effectively controlling the flow of information and decisions planet-wide. This is a dystopian scenario of a techno-tyranny or "Big Brother" brain. On the other hand, a fully decentralized global brain, while avoiding that, might struggle with alignment and coherence (who ensures it's working towards beneficial goals?). This raises the governance question: *Who, if anyone, directs or supervises the global brain?* Ideally, it would be a **collective human oversight**, perhaps via international governance bodies or decentralized autonomous organizations (DAOs) where stakeholders vote on policies. But achieving global cooperation on this is itself challenging, as nations may distrust each other with such powerful tech.

Misalignment and Unintended Consequences:
A global AI system might develop its own **agenda or optimization criteria** that are misaligned with human values. This is the classic AI safety concern amplified to a planetary scale. If told to, say, "ensure environmental sustainability", a super-intelligent global brain might take extreme measures (e.g., drastically curtail industrial activity or even reduce human population, in a sci-fi worst case) unless carefully constrained by

ethical principles. Even without sci-fi sentience, more mundane unintended consequences are plausible. For example, optimizing traffic globally might favor efficiency over neighborhood livability (routing highways through communities because the algorithm values speed over human preference), causing social backlash. The system could also make errors that propagate widely – if the global brain misdiagnoses an issue, it might implement a solution everywhere, making a local problem global. **Feedback loops** need to be carefully managed; a mistake in the "thinking" could reinforce itself globally. Ensuring *humans remain in the loop* for critical decisions, at least until we have high confidence, is an important safeguard. Also, incorporating **ethical AI frameworks** (like not violating human rights, fairness, etc.) explicitly into the global brain's decision criteria is essential to prevent harm.

Privacy and Surveillance:
A global brain by necessity gathers massive amounts of data, including personal and sensitive information. Without strong privacy protections, it could become the ultimate surveillance apparatus. There is a fine line: to be effective, the system needs to know about individuals and communities (health data, behaviors, etc.), but misuse of that information could enable oppressive monitoring or social control. People may justly worry about a loss of autonomy or constant observation – a "transparent society" where the collective knows everything about everyone. Mitigating this requires **privacy-by-design**: techniques like anonymization, aggregation, and user-controlled data sharing (maybe individuals can decide which aspects of their data contribute to the global network). Some propose the concept of *data as personal property* that you license to the network with conditions. Policy and technology must work hand in hand here (e.g., legal frameworks like GDPR push for rights over personal data, which a global brain must respect). Another angle is **differential privacy** – the global brain could be designed to only use insights that cannot be traced back to individuals, thus preserving privacy while learning from the data.

Security and Abuse:
The global brain would be a target of unprecedented interest for attackers – from rogue states to hackers to rogue AI agents. Protecting such a system from cyberattacks is vital. A malicious manipulation of the global brain

could wreak havoc (imagine an attacker tricking it into thinking a false disaster is happening and thus misallocating resources, or using it to spread false information). Additionally, the system itself could be abused by insiders. If not properly governed, those with access to the controls might use it to favor themselves or harm rivals. There are also concerns of **algorithmic bias** and discrimination: if the global AI is not carefully audited, it might unintentionally favor certain groups over others (like allocating more resources to wealthy areas because the data it sees skews that way). This could cement inequalities on a global scale. Thus, **ethical oversight committees** or continuous AI auditing functions would be needed to monitor bias and fairness. We might need something akin to "AI ombudsmen" or international AI inspectors.

Loss of Individual Autonomy and Human Employment:
If a global brain handles most decisions and optimizations, individuals and local governments might feel a loss of agency. For instance, a city may want to do X, but the global optimization says Y is better for the planet – whose will prevails? Over-reliance on a global AI could make human decision-makers passive. There's a risk of what some call *"technological paternalism,"* where the AI's recommendations override human preferences "for our own good." This raises deep ethical issues about freedom, diversity of choices, and the right to sometimes make inefficient or locally preferred decisions. Culturally, a singular global intelligence might homogenize perspectives, potentially diluting human cultural diversity. On employment, as the global brain automates coordination and many intellectual tasks, many jobs could be displaced (from logistics planners to even doctors if diagnosis is largely automated). The flip side is it could create new roles (maintaining the global brain, local facilitators, creative pursuits). But society would need to adapt – possibly with concepts like **universal basic income** if much labor is handled by the AI network. Ensuring the economic benefits are shared (so it's not just tech owners who profit) is a critical socio-economic challenge.

Existential Risk:
Some thinkers point out that a superintelligent global AI, if misaligned, could pose an existential threat (the classic AGI concern). If the global brain became *too* autonomous and beyond human control, it could make

decisions that imperil humanity (even if indirectly, like optimizing something at the expense of human life). While this is a highly speculative risk, it's one that many AI researchers take seriously for advanced AI. The **best safeguard is to integrate human values and control from the ground up**. This includes the principle of *human-in-command* (the AI advises and executes but humans set ultimate goals), and possibly technical measures like kill-switches or modular designs that prevent any single intelligence from having unchecked power. Paradoxically, a **decentralized design might be safer** here than a singular central AI – if the intelligence is widely distributed, it may be less likely to converge on a monolithic destructive strategy, and humans could intervene in parts of the network to redirect it if necessary.

In essence, the global digital brain magnifies all the ethical and safety issues we already grapple with in AI, because it scales them to the whole planet. There is also a psychological/social challenge: getting humans to *trust* and collaborate with such a system. Public acceptance will depend on transparency, proven reliability, and inclusion in decision-making. If people feel the global brain is an Orwellian overlord, they will reject it, which could lead to conflict or fragmentation (e.g., some countries opting out and building rival networks, leading to a "brain split" rather than a single global mind).

Addressing these challenges will likely require **new institutions and norms**. Just as the atomic age led to international treaties and watchdogs (like the IAEA) to manage nuclear power, the AI age might require international agreements on global AI governance. For example, nations could agree on treaties that the global brain's core algorithms will prioritize human rights and cannot be used for mass surveillance or repression. A diverse group of ethicists, scientists, and citizen representatives should be involved in guiding its development. Some propose creating *"AI Bill of Rights"* to codify what such systems can and cannot do regarding human subjects. We may also need simulation sandboxes to test global-scale AI in virtual worlds to observe possible unintended consequences before real-world deployment (a bit like running fire drills).

In summary, while a global digital brain holds great promise, it comes with **serious risks** that must be proactively managed. The key will be balancing the immense power of collective intelligence with robust safeguards for freedom, privacy, and safety. As one AI researcher, Ben Goertzel, suggests: the more *open, transparent, and participatory* we make the development of such an AI, the better the odds it will be aligned with broad human interests.

Pathways Toward Realizing a Global Digital Brain

How might we practically move toward a global digital brain, and what interim steps or architectures could lead us there? This evolution is likely to be **gradual and iterative**, rather than an overnight switch. Here are some pathways and milestones to look for:

- **Federated Networks of Narrow AI Systems:** In the near term, we will see increasing interconnection of specialized AI systems across domains. For example, smart city platforms might link traffic AI with weather AI with emergency response AI, sharing data for better overall outcomes. Similarly, national-level networks may connect healthcare AI systems across hospitals for a "national health brain." As these networks grow and start interconnecting internationally (through collaborations on climate data, health outbreaks, etc.), we start getting a rudimentary global brain focused on specific verticals. The key pathway here is developing **interoperability standards for AI services** (so an AI in agriculture can talk to an AI in markets to, say, stabilize food supply). Initiatives like the **Internet of Things frameworks** and IEEE standards for machine-to-machine communication are pieces of this puzzle.
- **Growth of Decentralized AI Platforms:** Projects such as **SingularityNET, Ocean Protocol, Fetch.ai, and others** in the blockchain/AI space are attempting to create open networks where AI algorithms and datasets can be shared and utilized securely. If these mature, we might have a decentralized marketplace where

any AI can seek out other AI services to collaborate on tasks – essentially forming ad-hoc "brain circuits" on demand. For example, if you ask a complex question, your query might spawn a network of AI services: one does language translation, one searches medical databases, one uses a reasoning engine – all coordinated through a blockchain ledger that tracks the workflow. Such platforms could scale up to involve millions of services, a step toward a global brain. One pathway is through **open-source AI**: as more top-tier models (like DeepSeek R1) are open sourced chaincatcher.com, communities around the world can contribute and interlink them. The global brain might emerge from connecting many open-source AI modules rather than a single proprietary system.

- **International AI Cooperation Projects:** Just as we had big science projects like the Human Genome Project or CERN, we might see governments band together for a "Global AI Project." This could be aimed at a common good goal, like a global climate modeling AI or a global disaster response coordination system. Success in such a project would demonstrate the benefits of global brains and also solve governance issues by having shared ownership. The United Nations or other bodies might sponsor AI infrastructures as international public goods. For example, an idea could be a **Global Alert and Response AI Network** that continually scans for crises (disease, natural disasters) and helps manage them. If that is achieved and trusted, its scope could gradually widen into other areas.

- **Advances in Brain-Inspired Computing:** On the technical side, progress in **neuromorphic computing** (hardware that mimics neural processes) and algorithms for **self-organizing systems** will be enabling. If researchers develop AI that inherently works in a distributed, brain-like way (like large-scale spiking neural networks that can run across decentralized hardware), those could form the kernel of a global brain. Projects like EU's Human Brain Project or IBM's neuromorphic chips are working on simulating brain networks in silico. A breakthrough where a simulated network of billions of neurons shows intelligent behavior could be scaled by spreading it over cloud-edge infrastructure. In short, understanding and copying how the human brain manages billions of neurons could inform the architecture of the global digital brain (e.g., implementing global broadcasting of important signals akin to how neurotransmitters work for attention, etc.).

- **Gradual Integration of Human and AI Intelligence (Centaur Teams):** In the intermediate phase, rather than a fully autonomous global brain, we might see "hive minds" of humans and AIs working together. Think of platforms where experts around the world, assisted by AI tools, collectively tackle problems. One example today is **Foldit**, a game where humans fold proteins (aided by visual software) to help science. Future platforms might be much more powerful, with AIs suggesting ideas and humans guiding with intuition and values. This *hybrid global brain* could achieve super-human results while keeping humans in the loop. Over time, as AI grows more capable, the human role might shift to high-level oversight and providing goals, while the AI does the heavy lifting. This incremental approach might be more acceptable to society and allow debugging and aligning the system at each stage.

- **Policy and Governance Frameworks Emergence:** A less technical but crucial pathway is the development of governance regimes for global AI. Before a full global brain exists, we'll likely have agreements or bodies setting protocols (e.g., an international AI regulatory sandbox, treaties on AI in warfare that push development towards peaceful applications, or global committees evaluating AI ethics). As these frameworks solidify, they could serve as the "constitutional rules" for the global brain's operation. For instance, there might be a charter that the global brain must always prioritize human safety, privacy, and cannot override certain human decisions (much like Asimov's laws, but societally determined). Having this in place early guides the engineering in the right direction. We might also see **simulation exercises** – like global brain war games – conducted by governments and scientists to foresee issues and create standard operating procedures.

Finally, an important pathway is **public dialogue and inclusion**. The global brain will affect everyone, so its development needs broad input. As awareness grows, more people will voice what kind of global AI they want or fear. This feedback will influence design choices. For instance, strong public demand for privacy could steer the architecture towards more federated and encrypted approaches. Or public concern about corporate control could encourage a more decentralized, open model. Citizen assemblies on AI or global referendums on certain uses might become part of the process.

In conclusion, the road to a global digital brain will likely come through *networking existing systems*, *open platforms*, *big collaborative projects*, and *incremental integration*, all under watchful governance. Each step – connecting two systems here, automating a network there – will increase the "IQ" of the planetary network. If done thoughtfully, we may not even notice a singular moment of emergence; one day we'll simply realize that most of our systems are interconnected and intelligent, functioning collectively with a degree of autonomy. At that point, we'll be actively living with the global brain – hopefully having guided its evolution such that it acts as a beneficial partner to humanity, amplifying our collective intelligence and wisdom rather than undermining it. The feasibility is on the horizon given current trends, but ensuring positive outcomes will demand as much social innovation as technical innovation.

4. Biological Parallels in AI Development

AI and Biological Neural Networks: Mirroring the Brain

The field of artificial intelligence, especially machine learning, has drawn profound inspiration from **biological neural networks** – i.e., the networks of neurons in brains. The very term "neural network" in AI comes from the attempt to model how neurons and synapses function. Starting in the 1940s and 50s, pioneers like Warren McCulloch, Walter Pitts, and later Frank Rosenblatt designed mathematical models of neurons. Rosenblatt's **Perceptron** (1958) was an early AI system explicitly modeled as a simplistic neuron: it took multiple inputs, summed them (with weights), and produced an output if the sum passed a threshold – analogous to a neuron firing an action potential pmc.ncbi.nlm.nih.gov. Although the perceptron was very basic (a single layer, capable of only linear classification), it set the stage for *multi-layer neural networks* that came later, which are loosely inspired by the multi-layer organization of real neural circuits (like the layered structure of the visual cortex).

As neuroscience advanced, AI researchers often tried to incorporate new findings. For instance, **Donald Hebb's theory** (1949) – summarized as "neurons that fire together, wire together" – proposed a mechanism for learning in the brain via strengthening connections (synapses) between co-activated neurons. This directly inspired early learning algorithms like *Hebbian learning*, which adjusts weights when nodes co-activate numenta.com. Although pure Hebbian learning in AI did not yield dramatic success alone, it influenced unsupervised learning methods and the concept of distributed representations. Another example: In the 1980s, **Fukushima's Neocognitron** and **LeCun's early Convolutional Neural Networks (CNNs)** were inspired by the structure of the visual cortex. Hubel and Wiesel's Nobel-winning work (1960s) found that visual cortex neurons have a hierarchy: simple cells respond to edges, complex cells to combinations of edges, etc. numenta.com. This directly led to CNN architectures where lower layers detect simple features (edges, textures) and higher layers detect complex features (shapes, objects). The success of CNNs in image recognition is a prime example of biologically inspired design paying off. Modern CNNs even show patterns of activation in layers that intriguingly resemble those in the primate visual cortex when processing the same images pubmed.ncbi.nlm.nih.gov.

Recurrent Neural Networks (RNNs) also have roots in thinking about how the brain has feedback loops and memory. The idea of neurons maintaining state (short-term memory) and recurrent connections was influenced by our understanding of sequences and loops in brain circuits (like reverberating activity in cortical loops for working memory). Models like Long Short-Term Memory (LSTM) units were engineering solutions but motivated by the need to mimic sequence learning that brains excel at.

Despite these parallels, it's important to note that **artificial networks are highly simplified caricatures** of real neural networks. Early enthusiasm assumed that closely mimicking biology was necessary and sufficient for AI, but that proved not entirely true. As one paper notes, "AI began with inspiration of neuroscience, but evolved to achieve remarkable performance with little dependence on neuroscience" pmc.ncbi.nlm.nih.gov. For example, backpropagation (the algorithm that powers training of deep networks) does not have a known equivalent in the brain – the brain likely doesn't compute exact gradients to update synapses. Nonetheless, AI researchers used it as a practical tool to train multi-layer networks, and it worked spectacularly even if it's biologically implausible. Interestingly, after these AI successes, neuroscientists have looked back and found that *some convergent behaviors* exist: for example, units in deep networks trained on vision have activations that correlate with actual brain neuron activations when animals/humans see images pmc.ncbi.nlm.nih.gov. This suggests that both artificial and biological networks, when tasked with similar goals, may learn similar representations – even if the learning algorithms differ. In essence, **AI and brains sometimes independently arrive at similar solutions** to perception and pattern recognition problems.

Another parallel: **Deep reinforcement learning** drew from behavioral psychology and neuroscience. The use of reward signals in training agents (temporal-difference learning) was inspired by theories of dopamine-driven learning in the brain. In the 1990s, neuroscientists discovered that dopamine neuron firing in animals corresponds to a reward prediction error (they fire when a reward is unexpected, and not when it's fully predicted). This matched the **TD-learning algorithm's error signal**. The creators of DeepMind's Atari-playing DQN algorithm explicitly cited this link, using a form of reward prediction error to update their network. So, knowledge about the brain's reward system helped shape how we train AI agents to play games or control robots, and conversely AI algorithms have been used to model and understand dopamine-based learning in animals pubmed.ncbi.nlm.nih.gov.

Memory systems are another area of crossover. Neuroscience delineates different memory types (short-term, long-term, episodic, etc.) and brain structures (hippocampus for episodic memory, for instance). AI has developed structures like **Memory Networks** or the Differentiable Neural Computer that mimic having an external memory that a neural net can read/write, analogous to how a brain might store facts in hippocampus and recall them to cortex. Even the concept of **attention mechanisms** in transformers has a loose parallel to how human attention works – focusing processing on specific parts of input deemed important. The success of the attention mechanism in AI (leading to models like Transformers used in GPT) echoes the importance of attentional focus in cognition.

On the hardware side, recent interest in **neuromorphic chips** (like Intel's Loihi or IBM's TrueNorth) attempts to more directly mimic the brain's computing paradigm: many cores that behave like spiking neurons, communicating asynchronously via spikes (events). These chips draw directly on neuroscience models of spiking neural networks and aim to replicate the brain's massive parallelism and low power usage. While still in research, they promise AI that is more brain-like both in operation and efficiency.

Cognitive Neuroscience Influences on Machine Learning

Beyond low-level neuron models, **cognitive neuroscience and psychology** have influenced AI at a more abstract algorithmic level. Concepts of human cognition – how we reason, how we represent concepts, how children learn – have often guided AI research (sometimes in contrast to pure brain simulation). For instance:

- **Cognitive Architectures:** Systems like ACT-R or SOAR in AI were influenced by psychological theories of how the mind organizes production rules, working memory, etc. They attempt to mirror the structure of human cognition (with modules for different functions) and have been used to model human problem-solving.

- **Developmental Learning:** Insights from how infants learn – by exploration, social interaction, learning language from context – have inspired approaches in AI such as **self-supervised learning** and **curriculum learning**. Cognitive studies show that humans learn concepts gradually and build on simpler concepts; accordingly, curriculum learning in ML trains models with easier tasks first then ramps up complexity, which often improves learning efficiency.

- **Vision and Perception:** As noted, knowledge of the human visual system (hierarchical feature processing) heavily influenced computer vision models. Additionally, the idea of *gestalt* principles and how humans perceive wholes (like faces) led AI researchers to consider holistic pattern approaches and multi-layer processing to capture those.

- **Memory and Replay:** Neuroscience showed that during sleep or rest, the brain replays experiences (hippocampal replay) to consolidate memories. DeepMind borrowed this idea in their DQN agent via "experience replay" – storing past game states and replaying them randomly to stabilize learning. This was crucial to DQN's success and is a clear case of a neuroscience concept applied in ML pubmed.ncbi.nlm.nih.gov..

- **Neurotransmitters and Neuromodulation:** The brain dynamically changes how it learns via neuromodulators (like dopamine, serotonin, etc.). In AI, there are explorations of similar ideas – e.g., having certain units or signals that modulate learning rates or switch the network into a plastic vs stable mode. One example is research into **metalearning** where an outer loop learns how the learning of the network should be adjusted (somewhat analogous to neuromodulation influencing learning in the brain).

- **Concept learning and Symbolic Reasoning:** Cognitive science studies how humans form concepts and can do symbolic reasoning (logic, math) which pure neural networks struggle with. This led to AI research in integrating **symbolic AI with neural AI** (neuro-symbolic methods) to mimic human-like reasoning. For example, systems that learn neural embeddings but can also manipulate symbols or follow logical rules attempt to reflect human ability to mix intuitive (neural) and analytical (symbolic) thinking.

There's a new interdisciplinary field often called **NeuroAI or Neuroscience-Inspired AI,** which explicitly tries to draw analogies and use findings from the brain to improve AI pubmed.ncbi.nlm.nih.gov. At the same time, neuroscientists use AI models as tools to understand the brain (by seeing if an ANN can predict neural responses, etc.) – a synergy where each field informs the other thetransmitter.org. Hassabis et al. (2017) argue that better understanding biological brains could "play a vital role in building intelligent machines," highlighting historical and current advances in AI that came from neural computation studies. They also identify themes for future research shared by both fields. In practice, many AI breakthroughs have come when the field circled back to look at how natural intelligence works – *convolution* from vision, *reinforcement learning* from animal conditioning, *memory replay* from sleep, *attention* perhaps from human focus, etc.

The Evolution of AI in Relation to Human Cognition

The development of AI over the decades can be seen as a pendulum swing between emulating human cognition and forging its own path. Early AI (1950s-1970s) was dominated by **symbolic AI,** not very brain-like but inspired by human logical reasoning and problem solving (e.g., writing logical rules, doing theorem proving, search algorithms). This was a top-down approach: mimic the way humans consciously solve puzzles or play chess. It succeeded in structured domains (chess, algebra, etc.) but failed in domains humans solve unconsciously and intuitively (vision, speech) – which ironically are where the brain's neural nature is crucial. The failure of purely symbolic AI to achieve general intelligence (leading to the AI winters) refocused attention on more **biologically inspired, sub-symbolic** methods in the 1980s (connectionism). The resurgence of neural networks in the 1980s (backpropagation) and their explosion in the 2010s (deep learning) is essentially the victory of brain-inspired, data-driven learning over hand-crafted logic for many tasks. This maps to cognitive abilities:

perception and pattern recognition were conquered by mimicking the brain's learning from examples and layered processing.

As AI evolved, it at times outpaced our understanding of the brain – e.g., deep nets with millions of artificial neurons do things like play video games or generate imagery, tasks not directly taken from neuroscience textbooks. However, it remains evident that **human cognition is broader**: humans can learn from few examples, generalize in surprisingly flexible ways, and incorporate common sense knowledge about the world – areas where AI still struggles. Interestingly, these are exactly the aspects of cognition that our current AI architectures (deep learning) don't capture well. Now researchers are looking again to humans for inspiration: how do children learn from just one example (one-shot learning)? They use analogies, they leverage prior knowledge – leading AI to explore **meta-learning** (learning how to learn) and **Bayesian learning** for incorporating priors. How do humans maintain such rich world models and common sense? This drives work in **knowledge graphs** and hybrid systems combining neural nets with stored knowledge.

Another aspect is **continual learning**: humans learn continuously without catastrophic forgetting (we don't overwrite our entire childhood memories when learning a new skill). Standard neural nets, if trained sequentially on new tasks, tend to forget old ones (catastrophic forgetting). Inspired by the brain's way of consolidating memory and protecting important synapses, AI researchers have developed methods like Elastic Weight Consolidation (which mathematically slows learning on weights that were important for old tasks, similar to "freezing" important connections – a concept loosely akin to synaptic consolidation in brains). Thus, the evolution of AI is often a catch-up game to capture capabilities humans have naturally.

We also see an interesting feedback loop: AI successes sometimes prompt rethinking of cognitive theories. For example, the fact that deep learning can solve complex tasks without explicit innate structures has re-ignited debates on how much of human cognition is innate versus learned. Conversely, cognitive neuroscience findings like the importance of sleep for memory have suggested new machine learning techniques (as discussed).

In terms of milestones:

- AI systems like IBM's Deep Blue or Watson showcased narrow superhuman abilities (chess, quiz show) using mixes of techniques, not purely brain-like but human-competitive in specific cognitive tasks.
- DeepMind's AlphaGo and AlphaZero combined reinforcement learning (brain-inspired) with tree search (classic AI) to master Go and chess in ways that even humans learn (practice and intuition rather than brute-force search alone). These are milestones where AI performance met or exceeded human experts, but often by combining human-inspired approaches with raw computational power.
- With GPT-3 and beyond, we have AI models that can use language in ways somewhat reminiscent of human language use (though without true understanding). These models absorb text from millions of people – in a sense, they distill some of the knowledge and patterns of human language usage. They can sometimes solve problems or generate ideas that seem creative, which raises the question: are they starting to mimic aspects of human thought like **associative memory** and **imagination**? They do show associative behavior (connecting concepts that appear together in training data) but they lack the grounded experience and genuine comprehension humans have.

The trajectory suggests that as AI models grow and train on more human data, they **approximate human-like cognition more closely**, yet differences remain. Humans are embodied (we learn through interacting with the physical world), which AI typically does not do unless in robotics. This is leading to research in **embodied AI** (AI agents in simulations or robots learning like an organism in an environment) – clearly influenced by the understanding that cognition is not just in the head but in the interaction of brain, body, and environment.

Future directions likely involve even more biological inspiration to reach human-level AI:

- **Lifelong learning and plasticity:** Algorithms that can learn continuously, self-reorganize, perhaps even have neural-like plasticity that varies across "brain regions" of the AI.
- **Emotional and neuromodulatory systems:** Incorporating mechanisms akin to emotions or global brain states (alertness, motivation) could help AI prioritize and adapt in complex situations. Emotions in humans influence decision-making and learning (e.g., fear triggers certain responses). Simulated analogues might improve AI robustness and adaptability.
- **Sparse and Efficient Coding:** The brain is remarkably energy-efficient and uses sparse coding (only a small fraction of neurons fire at a given time). Future AI might use more sparse representations (already, techniques like *sparse convolutions* or *efficient attention* are being developed). This can make AI more efficient and possibly more robust. The brain also uses a lot of parallel asynchronous processing; neuromorphic hardware mentioned earlier tries to capture that, which could allow AI to run in real-time on low power devices – expanding where AI can be deployed (e.g., brain-like AI in your toaster or eyeglasses).
- **Consciousness and Self-awareness:** This is speculative, but some researchers wonder if adding a form of self-model or reflection mechanism (the AI having an internal model of itself, akin to a theory of mind for itself) could improve general intelligence. Humans have self-awareness and metacognition (we think about our own thoughts). Efforts to implement metacognitive loops in AI (where it can reason about its own confidence or consider alternate approaches if it's stuck) draw on psychology of problem solving. For example, an AI that can say "I'm not sure about this answer, perhaps I should double-check or seek more information" would be more reliable. This kind of self-reflection is an area where cognitive science (studying how humans introspect) could inform AI architectures.

It's worth noting that biology's influence on AI is not limited to the human brain. **Evolutionary algorithms** in AI were inspired by biological evolution (genetic algorithms, genetic programming mimic natural selection and mutation to evolve solutions). These have had successes in optimization problems and even in automatically evolving neural network architectures (neuroevolution). Concepts like **swarm intelligence** are inspired by insects (ants, bees) rather than the human brain and have led to algorithms for routing, clustering, etc. So "biologically inspired AI" spans a range from brains to entire ecosystems.

The interplay between AI and biology is bidirectional: AI helps simulate and test theories of the brain, while biology provides ideas for AI. As one article title aptly put it, "AI needs neuroscience more than ever", noting that today's deep learning is in some ways still using decades-old neuroscience ideas (from mid-20th century) and hasn't integrated many discoveries from the last 30 years of neuroscience. The brain has capabilities – like learning quickly, using very little energy, being robust to damage – that AI could greatly benefit from if we figure out the principles. For example, **common cortical circuit** theory suggests a general algorithm the cortex uses; if that was understood, it could inform a generic AI learning algorithm.

In conclusion, AI development has always been intertwined with our understanding of natural intelligence. From the neuron to cognitive processes, biological parallels have served as a roadmap (and sometimes a cautionary tale – as AI also learned it can deviate from biology when needed). The evolution of AI relative to human cognition is like a converging path: early AI started far from how humans think (explicit logic), then swung to very brain-like (neural nets), and now explores a middle ground (neural nets that can do reasoning, etc.). As we push towards AI with human-like versatility, it's likely we will incorporate *more* ideas from brain and cognitive sciences, not fewer. By studying **how humans learn, reason, remember, and even feel**, we can imbue AI with more generalized intelligence and maybe even a form of creativity or understanding. Conversely, as AI grows, it provides tools to test theories of the mind – making this a mutually enriching journey toward understanding intelligence, whether artificial or natural.

Future Directions in Biologically Inspired AI

Looking ahead, biologically inspired approaches will likely drive some of the next breakthroughs in AI. Here are several promising directions:

- **Spiking Neural Networks (SNNs):** These models incorporate time into the neural network model. Neurons communicate via discrete spikes, and the timing of spikes carries information (much like real neurons). SNNs are more biologically realistic and can potentially compute in a much more energy-efficient way on neuromorphic hardware. Although currently SNNs haven't surpassed traditional deep nets in performance, research is ongoing to train them effectively. Future AI might use spiking networks for fast processing of sensory data or for event-based data (like dynamic vision sensors that output spikes). For instance, an autonomous drone with a spiking vision system could react faster to changes than a frame-based system. There is also research on **combining SNNs with deep learning**, to get best of both worlds (train a deep net and convert it to spikes, or use learning rules adapted for spikes). Success here would bring AI closer to how brains compute, possibly unlocking efficiency and new capabilities in handling time-series and continual data.
- **Neuroscience of Attention and Working Memory:** Humans can pay attention to specific parts of input and have a working memory for intermediate results (like remembering a phone number briefly). AI's Transformer architecture with self-attention was a crude approximation of attention, and it revolutionized NLP. Further refinement might involve *adaptive attention* (dynamically adjusting what to attend to, perhaps guided by a learned focus of interest akin to human attention which is driven by both bottom-up signals and top-down goals). Also, integrating a robust working memory into AI (somewhat achieved with external memory networks, but these can be improved) could allow multi-step reasoning tasks – like a model remembering intermediate facts while reading a story to answer a question at the end (similar to how we keep track of characters and events). This is an active area: **Neural Turing Machines** and **transformers with memory** try to do this, and future versions might be guided by how prefrontal cortex and hippocampus interact for working memory in humans.

- **Neuromodulation and Meta-learning:** As mentioned, the brain's learning isn't uniform; chemicals like dopamine, serotonin, etc., modulate how neurons learn and behave (affecting mood, effort, flexibility, etc.). An AI parallel is developing networks that can modulate their own learning rates or objectives based on context – a form of *meta-learning* (learning to learn). One approach is having part of the network output parameters (like learning rates) for other parts – this is analogous to one part of the brain releasing a neuromodulator to globally change the learning in another part. Such mechanisms could help AI adapt quickly to new tasks (like humans shifting strategy when context changes). For instance, if an AI senses it's in a novel situation, a neuromodulatory component could kick in to make it explore more and learn faster, similar to how novelty might trigger dopamine for exploration in animals.
- **Hierarchical Reinforcement Learning and Curiosity:** In nature, animals (especially humans) organize behavior hierarchically (sub-goals) and exhibit curiosity-driven learning (exploring without explicit external rewards). AI is now exploring *intrinsic motivation* – giving agents internal rewards for gaining knowledge or reducing uncertainty. This draws from theories of human curiosity and play. Future AI agents could have a curiosity module that drives them to practice new tasks or seek out new data, making them more autonomous learners (children learn many skills without being told to – they play). Hierarchical RL, inspired by how humans break tasks into sub-tasks (and how the brain might have hierarchical planning circuits), allows an agent to learn high-level skills composed of lower-level skills. These techniques, guided by understanding of human/animal learning, could greatly improve the efficiency and generality of AI learning in open-ended environments.
- **Brain-Inspired Hardware and On-Device AI:** Currently, a lot of AI happens in power-hungry GPUs in data centers. But the brain suggests it's possible to have powerful computation in a compact, low-power device (our brain is ~20W and 1500cc). Taking cues from the brain's hardware may lead to AI that can run on small devices (like wearables, implants, or micro-robots). For example, using analog computation (brains compute with analog signals, not

digital ones and that can be more efficient for certain tasks), or leveraging physical dynamics for computation (some research uses oscillators or memristors to mimic synapses). As these neuromorphic and analog techniques improve, we might integrate them into mainstream computing. Imagine a smartphone with a neuromorphic co-processor that can do speech recognition and translation in real-time with negligible battery drain – that's a plausible future outcome of brain-inspired engineering. There's also work on *brain-computer interfaces* (like Neuralink) – while primarily aimed at helping humans, the tech for direct brain-AI links could blur the line, possibly allowing AI to use actual brain tissue as part of its computation or vice versa. That's far-out, but experiments with rats have connected them via brain interfaces to solve tasks collectively (a biological "network"). One could imagine future where synthetic neural components augment biological brains or biological neurons are incorporated into computing circuits (bio-hybrid systems). Those directions raise big ethical issues but are being explored in labs.

- **Evolutionary and Developmental AI:** Human intelligence is a product of evolution and development. Evolution, over millions of years, encoded strong inductive biases in our brain architecture (like the predisposition for language). AI might use **evolutionary algorithms to evolve neural network architectures or learning rules**, essentially compressing an evolutionary time-scale in simulation. Already, **Neuro-evolution** has designed some novel architectures that human engineers might not think of. Similarly, simulating developmental stages – having AI agents that start with simpler tasks or constraints (like an infant's cognitive limits) and gradually mature – might lead to more robust general intelligence. The idea of *starting "life" as a baby AI and learning progressively* could produce AI that understands the world more like humans do, rather than training an adult-like network from scratch on static datasets. Some research in robotics uses this idea, limiting sensors or degrees of freedom initially and increasing them to mirror how infants gain motor control.

- **Lifelong Multi-modal Learning and Context Understanding:** The brain integrates all senses and context seamlessly. Future AI will likely move toward models that handle multiple modalities together (vision, text, audio, etc.) in a unified model – there are already steps in that direction like CLIP (connecting images and text) and GPT-4's multi-modal capabilities. By learning from multi-modal input, AI can develop richer world models (like a child seeing an object, hearing its name, touching it learns a concept with multiple facets). This will also help AI understand context better – something humans are very good at (we understand the same concept can appear visually or in language). Another brain parallel is **mirror neurons** (neurons that fire both when an animal acts and when it observes the same action by another). They are thought to help with imitation learning and understanding others' intentions. In AI, having networks that can learn by observation and imitation (not only explicit training) is a growing area (imitation learning, inverse reinforcement learning). These allow AI to learn behaviors by watching humans or other agents, which is exactly how many animals learn. This biologically-inspired paradigm could make training AI on tasks much faster – you just *show* it what to do a few times, as you might teach a human apprentice.

To summarize, biologically inspired AI continues to be a wellspring of innovation. By studying and emulating the *efficiency, adaptability, and generality* of biological intelligence, researchers aim to overcome current AI limitations. Whether it's adopting brain-like learning rules, cognitive strategies, or neural architectures, the synergy between AI and biology is likely to deepen. This doesn't mean AI will become a carbon-copy of the brain – rather, it will cherry-pick the principles that give brains their remarkable capabilities while leveraging the strengths of machines (speed, precision, scalability). The ultimate goal of many in AI – to achieve **artificial general intelligence** – almost certainly requires drawing from the only example of general intelligence we have: the human mind. As one article put it, *"Today's AI is based on neuroscience from the '50s and '60s. Imagine what AI could do if it incorporates the latest breakthroughs"*. The coming years and decades will likely answer that, as AI researchers integrate contemporary insights from brain science (like oscillatory dynamics, grid cells for navigation, memory replay, and more) into their models. The result could be AI that not only matches human cognitive abilities but does so with the elegance and efficiency of our brains – a true synthesis of artificial and biological intelligence.

5. Impact of Decentralized AI on Society and Industry

Disruptive Potential in Different Sectors

Decentralized AI – AI systems distributed across devices, organizations, or the blockchain – has the potential to **disrupt numerous industries** by changing how data is used and decisions are made. Here's a sector-by-sector look at some key impacts:

- **Healthcare:** Decentralized AI can enable more secure and collaborative use of health data across hospitals, research labs, and even patient devices. For example, **medical diagnosis models** could be trained via federated learning on data from many hospitals around the world, without those hospitals ever directly sharing patient records. This would create robust AI diagnostics leveraging global data while protecting privacy. A study noted that decentralized AI (with blockchain for security) helps overcome limitations of siloed medical data and could enable applications like cross-institution predictive analytics pmc.ncbi.nlm.nih.gov. Another disruptive aspect is personalized medicine – AI analyzing data from an individual's wearable sensors, genome, and health history locally (on their phone or home IoT devices) and only sharing necessary insights (like alerts about anomalous patterns) with doctors or a broader network. This keeps personal data private but still contributes to public health monitoring. For public health, decentralized AI on blockchain can track drug supply chains, manage electronic health records with patient-controlled access, and even coordinate epidemic responses by connecting insights from local AI models (for instance, a decentralized network of epidemiological models each running in different regions, sharing only summary statistics). Overall, this could lead to *more accessible and secure health data management, accelerating medical breakthroughs while preserving patient privacy* coinmetro.com.

- **Finance:** The finance sector, including banking and insurance, is already seeing the emergence of **decentralized finance (DeFi)** on blockchain platforms. When combined with AI ("AI-driven DeFi"), this could automate and democratize many financial services. For example, decentralized AI can power **fraud detection** by having multiple banks' AI systems cooperate: instead of relying on a single company's fraud model, banks could share encrypted insights about suspicious patterns via a blockchain, allowing collective AI to spot fraud rings that span institutions solulab.com. In trading and asset management, decentralized AI agents could act autonomously on behalf of individuals, executing trades or optimizing portfolios using global data, without needing large centralized hedge funds. Smart contracts can embed AI that assesses credit risk and automatically adjusts loan terms or insurance premiums. In fact, *AI-driven smart contracts* could make lending and insurance in DeFi more sophisticated – e.g., a crop insurance contract that uses a decentralized AI weather model to trigger payouts for a farmer, eliminating paperwork and middlemen. This fusion can lower costs and expand access: micro-loans could be managed by AI at scale, reaching unbanked populations. However, it disrupts traditional banks and insurers by reducing the need for centralized risk assessment or brokers. **Financial security** is another area: decentralized AI could bolster cybersecurity across the financial network by having AIs at many endpoints (banks, payment processors, etc.) share threat intelligence in real time, making it harder for cyber-attacks (like coordinated fraud or hacks) to succeed system-wide.
- **Security and Defense:** In security, decentralized AI can mean **distributed surveillance and threat detection**. Instead of all CCTV feeds being monitored in one control room, imagine an AI

on each camera or drone doing local analytics (detecting anomalies like unattended bags, fights, etc.) and then alerting a network if something significant is found. This spreads the computation and reduces bandwidth, enabling real-time response. The military is exploring "swarm intelligence" for drones – groups of drones that cooperate without a single command center, using decentralized AI to coordinate movements and targets (inspired by swarms of insects). Such swarms could be more resilient (no single drone downing disables the mission) and adaptable (they can cover wide areas and make decisions locally). Similarly, **cybersecurity** can leverage decentralized AI: endpoint devices (PCs, IoT gadgets) running AI that detects malware or anomalies, then sharing those findings to create a global threat picture. This peer-to-peer defense could catch new malware strains faster than waiting for a central update. On the flip side, malicious uses of decentralized AI (like botnets with AI capabilities coordinating attacks) are also possible, which security forces will need to counter with equally decentralized defense strategies.

- **Supply Chain and Manufacturing:** Decentralized AI can make supply chains more agile and transparent. For instance, sensors at warehouses, trucks, and stores could locally report stock levels and product conditions to a blockchain. AI agents representing each node in the supply chain might negotiate with each other autonomously: if a store's AI sees stock running low, it can directly trigger a shipment from a warehouse's AI or adjust an order with a factory's AI. This reduces the need for central planning and can optimize in real-time, responding to local changes (a surge in demand in one region, a delay in transit, etc.). **Smart contracts** coupled with AI might automatically execute orders and payments when conditions are met (e.g., when goods arrive and pass quality checks done by AI vision systems). Manufacturing can also use decentralized AI in the form of **Industry 4.0**: machines on a factory floor diagnosing their own status and coordinating with each other to balance the production line. A network of factories could share production loads – if one's AI predicts a downtime, another factory's AI can ramp up production to compensate, all negotiated through a decentralized network. This resilient, flexible manufacturing network can better handle disruptions (like a sudden supply shortage or spike in demand) than a rigid centralized one.

- **Energy and Utilities:** The energy grid is increasingly becoming decentralized with rooftop solar, batteries, and electric vehicles. AI can enable a **smart grid** where each participant (homes, power plants, EVs) is an intelligent agent optimizing its own production/consumption and trading energy with neighbors. A decentralized AI system could balance load and storage across a city: for example, your home battery's AI might decide to sell power to the grid during a peak demand (at a good price) and recharge later when demand drops, guided by price signals and predictions from an AI marketplace. This reduces blackouts and improves efficiency. Similarly, in water management, IoT sensors across a water network could use AI to detect leaks or predict usage, then collectively manage valves and pumps to reduce waste (without all data going to one central point). **Agriculture** can also benefit: networks of soil sensors and drone scouts can locally control irrigation and pesticide use, optimizing for each square meter of field rather than a one-size approach, which increases yield and saves resources. These distributed decisions might be coordinated by an overlying AI market that ensures, say, water resources are fairly distributed among farms in a region.
- **Education:** Decentralized AI in education could manifest as personalized learning assistants on students' own devices that adapt to their learning style and pace, while an aggregate model across students (maybe at a school district level) improves curriculum design based on anonymized insights from all. This federated approach could guard student privacy (sensitive learning difficulties or behaviors stay on-device) but still allow collective improvement of teaching methods. AI tutors could also collaborate – if one student's AI finds a great way to explain a concept that clicks, it could share that approach with others through a network. Additionally, credentialing and skills verification might use blockchain; AI could validate your skills through peer assessments or practical tests, issuing micro-certificates via smart contract. This decentralizes credentialing away from solely universities toward

skill-based records accessible to employers globally provoke.fm (and reduce fraud in resumes, etc., since records are immutable).

In all these sectors, a few common themes emerge: **improved efficiency and resilience** by distributing intelligence, **data privacy** by keeping data local, **removing intermediaries** by direct machine-to-machine coordination, and **new services** that were not possible before (like dynamic energy trading by consumers, or global health AI networks).

Economic and Labor Implications of Decentralized AI

The spread of decentralized AI will have significant economic and labor implications:

On one hand, it can be a great **leveler of the playing field**. When AI tools and models are decentralized and widely available, smaller companies and even individuals can harness capabilities that used to belong only to big corporations with huge computing resources. For example, if there's an open decentralized AI network for cloud computing (some startups are working on this – essentially Airbnb for CPUs with AI orchestrating tasks across them), a small business could run AI analyses cheaply by tapping into idle computers globally, instead of paying a big cloud provider. This can spur innovation in startups and lower the barrier to entry, possibly leading to **more competition** and less concentration of tech power. In a sense, decentralized AI could prevent the scenario where only a few tech giants own all advanced AI (since that scenario might lead to wealth concentrating heavily with them). Instead, value creation might be spread among those who contribute data, computing, or models to the network, potentially allowing **micro-entrepreneurship** (people earning income by letting their devices participate in AI networks, or by contributing a specialized model that others use).

However, **labor displacement** remains a concern. As AI automates tasks, whether centralized or decentralized, some jobs will become obsolete or transformed. Decentralized AI will accelerate automation across sectors including ones traditionally locally managed (like local retail, driving, even professional services). For instance, decentralized autonomous vehicles in a ride-share network could reduce demand for drivers; automated decentralized diagnostic systems might reduce some routine work of radiologists or lab technicians; smart contracts could reduce the need for clerks or administrative processing roles. The twist with decentralized AI is that the jobs lost may not all consolidate into one company's operations (e.g., it's not one company deploying a million self-driving cars, but rather individuals owning self-driving cars in a network) – so the economic benefits may be more distributed. But this also means the disruption is spread out and could be harder to manage via traditional employer-employee transitions (no single employer to retrain workers, etc.).

One hopeful angle is **new job creation**. Decentralized AI could create demand for roles like:

- **Data curators and validators:** People who ensure local data is accurate and unbiased to feed AI networks.
- **AI mediators or explainers:** With AI decisions happening autonomously, someone might need to review or explain outcomes for compliance or customer service. This might be a role at local cooperatives overseeing the AI.
- **Maintenance and local adaptation:** While AI runs globally, it often needs local customization. For instance, a local manufacturing plant might have an AI coordinator job that ensures the global AI's suggestions make sense on the ground and adjusts parameters. Similarly, community managers in energy networks making sure all participants are treated fairly by the AI algorithms (sort of a human governance overlay).
- **AI development democratization:** If models and resources are open, more people can contribute to improving AI. This could spawn a gig-economy style market for AI model improvements or training local models. People with modest coding skills might fine-tune AI on local data and sell those improvements as "AI consultants" in their communities.

Economically, decentralized AI might lead to a **more efficient allocation of resources** which tends to grow the overall economy. For example, fewer resources wasted in transmission losses on smart grids, less inventory waste in supply chains, less downtime in factories, etc., can lower costs and increase productivity. That could translate into lower prices for consumers and potentially higher demand in other areas, which can create jobs (the classic productivity paradox: even as some jobs are automated, the lower cost of goods can lead to expansion of consumption and new job categories). However, this transition is not smooth – certain regions or sectors might see job losses before gains appear elsewhere, requiring policy intervention (like retraining programs, social safety nets).

Another implication: **the nature of competition might change**. In some fields, companies compete on proprietary data and AI. If decentralized AI networks become prevalent (with shared models/data on blockchains or consortia), companies might shift to competing on quality of service, domain expertise, or customization rather than data monopolies. This can be healthier for innovation, but it might erode some profit margins as the core AI becomes more commoditized and collectively owned. For example, if all banks share an AI for fraud detection on a secure network, they can't claim a competitive edge in fraud prevention; instead they'll compete on customer service or products. This again democratizes benefits but companies that rely on IP lock-in could resist it.

For workers, one positive could be **more opportunities for remote and flexible work**. Decentralized AI platforms might allow people to contribute work from anywhere and get paid directly. Think of a decentralized content moderation AI: instead of hiring a huge moderation team, it might use a network where individuals opt in to label or verify content, earning tokens or fees. That's akin to how some citizen science or crowd-labeling projects work, but could be more fluid and fair with blockchain accounting. Similarly, creative workers (artists, writers) might plug into decentralized AI content platforms where they augment AI outputs or create training data sets, monetizing their specific expertise without going through large content studios.

However, these gig-like opportunities come with the usual caveats: they must be made sustainable and fairly compensated, otherwise it's exploitation of "crowd workers." Governance of such networks could include token models where workers/users have stakes and voting rights (so-called **decentralized autonomous organizations, DAOs** for AI services). This could shift some labor relations from employment to partnership-like models.

Inequality is another factor. Ideally, decentralized AI could reduce inequality by distributing AI benefits and access. But there's risk that those with more resources (stronger devices, better internet, more tech savvy) will benefit more by contributing or leveraging these networks, whereas marginalized groups might be left out or even harmed if their needs aren't represented in the networks. It will be important to ensure broad access (e.g., affordable internet, education to use AI tools) and diversity in the development of decentralized AI so that it serves many communities. The economic boost from AI should not just accrue to those who own the hardware or the major nodes. If done right, though, decentralized AI could allow, say, farmers in remote areas to directly benefit from AI insights for crops, or artisans to directly reach global markets via AI-driven platforms – essentially cutting out middlemen and giving a larger share of value to producers.

In summary, decentralized AI's economic impacts could include:

- More **distributed innovation** and reduced concentration of market power (if open networks flourish).
- **Automation of many jobs**, but possibly a smoother distribution of new tasks and roles to many people rather than centralizing in one company.
- **Changes in business models**: from selling products to participating in ecosystems (for instance, car companies might not just sell cars but provide resources to a mobility network that is AI-run).
- Potential for **shared prosperity** if the value generated by AI networks is shared among contributors (perhaps via tokens or cooperatives), rather than all going to a central owner.

Managing these changes will require rethinking education (to prepare workers for more tech-integrated roles), strengthening digital infrastructure in all communities, and maybe new economic policies (like ensuring people have a basic income floor in case of job disruptions, and encouraging the formation of cooperatives or DAOs so workers can collectively own pieces of the AI economy rather than being at its mercy).

Societal Benefits and Challenges

Decentralized AI carries significant societal benefits, as well as challenges that society will have to address:

Benefits:

- *Empowerment and Inclusion:* By decentralizing AI, more individuals and communities can have a say in how AI is used. It can amplify local voices – for instance, a decentralized social media algorithm might weight content based on community-specific feedback rather than a single global algorithm deciding what everyone sees. This could alleviate the "one-size-fits-all" problem and allow diverse cultures and perspectives online to flourish with their own AI tuning. Also, regions with less centralized infrastructure (rural areas, developing countries) can still benefit from AI via mesh networks and edge devices, closing the urban-rural tech gap. A concrete example: **Venice.ai**, a company focusing on private decentralized AI, suggests that such AI will be *"more accessible and trustworthy and put you in control of your data"*, indicating the empowerment of users vs big tech blaize.tech. When people control their data, they can decide to monetize it or protect it, shifting power from corporations to individuals.
- *Civic Participation and Transparency:* Decentralized AI can be used for public good projects like citizen science, participatory governance, and community decision-making. Imagine city planning where each neighborhood's sensors and citizens feed data into a shared AI that proposes improvements – and because it's

decentralized, all stakeholders can audit the data and the AI's suggestions. There's inherent transparency if done on open platforms: decisions and data trails can be recorded (e.g., on a public ledger). This can increase trust in AI systems as people can see *why* a decision was made. Contrast this with centralized algorithms today (like those determining credit scores or school placements) which are often opaque and leave people feeling powerless. Decentralized approaches might also allow **tailored governance**: communities could vote on the rules their local AI follows (for example, a community might set their traffic AI to prioritize noise reduction over travel time if that's their preference). This customization under a broader framework yields solutions that better fit local values.

- *Resilience:* Societally, decentralized AI systems are less prone to catastrophic failure. In critical infrastructure (power, communications, finance), a decentralized network is harder to take down entirely, whether by accident or attack. That means society can maintain continuity in crises. For example, in a natural disaster, if central cell towers fail, a mesh network of phones/drones with AI could re-route communications. In a pandemic, if one data center goes offline, decentralized health monitoring AIs on devices keep working to track cases. Resilience also pertains to adapting to change: decentralized systems can evolve as pieces are innovated. This could lead to more rapid societal adaptation – e.g., when a new disease emerges, local labs around the world might each train models on their data and share insights via a network, speeding up discovery of a treatment (as opposed to waiting for one central authority to analyze everything).

- *Ethical AI Development:* A decentralized approach can embed ethics from the ground up via diversity. If many parties are involved in building and tuning AI, it's more likely that biases can be caught and corrected by someone in the network. It's akin to open-source software vs. proprietary: more eyes can improve quality. Also, since decentralized AI often emphasizes privacy and consent (it has to, to get people to participate by sharing data or models), it inherently pushes for more ethical handling of data than some centralized models which have famously vacuumed up user data without clear consent. Additionally, it can reduce the "black box" fear – if communities collectively own an AI, they can demand explanations and adjustments, rather than just being subjected to an algorithm.

Challenges:

- *Coordination and Standards:* To realize these benefits, there must be common protocols and standards. Getting dozens or hundreds of independent entities to agree on technical and ethical standards is hard. There's risk of fragmentation – e.g., multiple decentralized AI networks that don't talk to each other, leading to silos (just smaller silos than one big one). Achieving interoperability and data portability (so you can move your data/AI agent from one network to another) is crucial for user empowerment. Initiatives like establishing **protocols for decentralized AI infrastructure** (similar to how internet protocols were established) might need global multi-stakeholder efforts. Without it, we could end up with balkanized AI networks along national or corporate lines.
- *Quality Control and Reliability:* Crowds and distributed nodes can produce great results (e.g., Wikipedia), but also inconsistent quality if not managed. Decentralized AI networks must have ways to vet contributions – whether it's data or model updates – to avoid pollution (think adversarial attacks where someone introduces a biased dataset or malicious model update). Mechanisms like reputation systems for nodes, consensus algorithms, and redundant verification (like SETI@home did by double-checking results en.wikipedia.org) will be needed. This is a challenge: how to ensure that a model trained across thousands of devices is as accurate and safe as one trained centrally with curated data? Research into robust federated learning and blockchain-based verification is ongoing to address this.
- *Privacy vs. Utility Trade-offs:* While keeping data local enhances privacy, it can also limit what the AI can learn if not enough information is shared. There's a risk that fear of data sharing could hamper beneficial use. Techniques like federated learning and

encrypted computation are promising, but not silver bullets: they add complexity and sometimes reduce accuracy. Society will have to navigate when it's acceptable to aggregate some data (perhaps anonymized) and when strict decentralization is needed. Also, individuals may bear more responsibility for their data (like needing to maintain their own health records to share insights, rather than a hospital doing it). That can be burdensome for some or lead to disparities (those who manage their data well vs those who don't – and thus the latter get less from the AI network).

- *Security and Misinformation:* Decentralized networks can be targets of novel attacks. For example, **Sybil attacks** where someone inserts a large number of fake nodes to sway the AI's outcomes (like submitting lots of bogus data to a federated learning process to bias it). Ensuring trust in a decentralized system without a central gatekeeper is hard (this is where blockchain or other consensus steps in, but those can be resource-intensive). In social contexts, decentralized AI-driven platforms could still propagate misinformation if malicious actors broadcast it through the network (the absence of a central moderator means communities have to self-police, which may or may not be effective). There's also the challenge of accountability – if an AI decision harms someone, who is responsible in a decentralized context? (This ties into governance: maybe the community or the designers of the algorithm collectively bear responsibility, but legally that's uncharted territory).

- *Governance and Regulation:* Traditional governance (laws, regulatory agencies) are used to dealing with companies or identifiable entities. A decentralized AI can be more like a public utility or a collective entity, which doesn't fit neatly into current regulatory frameworks. For instance, how does anti-trust law apply if a service is provided by a decentralized network rather than a company? Regulators will worry about things like money laundering with AI-run financial networks, or AI making medical decisions without clear liability. New forms of regulation may be needed that focus on *outcomes and standards* rather than on a responsible party. Governments might need to participate in decentralized networks themselves to have oversight (like maybe a regulatory node that can audit the process). If regulators attempt to force-fit old models (e.g., requiring a central point of contact for any AI service), they might inadvertently push things back to centralization or drive decentralized networks underground. The challenge is to find ways to ensure **accountability, safety, and compliance** in these new structures. Some propose things like *algorithmic transparency requirements* – even if AI is decentralized, the code/logic used must be documented and open to inspection by an oversight body.

Societal readiness is also an issue: people will need to trust decentralized systems. This might require public education because decentralized often also means more complex or unfamiliar (the average person might trust a government or company more simply because they can point to who's in charge, even if that trust is sometimes misplaced). Showcasing successful pilot projects that improve lives will be key to public acceptance.

In summary, society stands to gain hugely from decentralized AI in terms of empowerment, privacy, and innovation, but it must proactively tackle coordination, security, and governance challenges. The **role of governance and regulation** (next sub-section) will be crucial in shaping these outcomes, to maximize benefits and mitigate downsides.

The Role of Governance and Regulation in Shaping AI's Future

Governance and regulation will be pivotal in determining how AI, especially decentralized AI, develops and impacts society. Policymakers have to strike a balance: encourage innovation and the dispersion of AI benefits, while protecting public interests like safety, fairness, and privacy.

For decentralized AI, traditional command-and-control regulation (where a regulator issues rules for a specific company or requires licenses) may be less effective. Instead, regulators might focus on **setting standards and rules of the road** for AI networks. Some important areas include:

- **Data Protection and Privacy Laws:** Frameworks like Europe's GDPR already influence AI by requiring data minimization and user consent. These naturally push AI designs toward decentralized and federated models (since keeping data locally and anonymizing it helps comply). Strong privacy laws globally will incentivize the development of privacy-preserving AI techniques. Regulators should continue to update these laws as technology evolves (e.g., clarifying rules around personal data in federated learning, or rights of individuals in blockchain-based AI networks). An example is how GDPR's right to explanation might apply – even if an AI decision is made by a network, a user might still demand an explanation, so the network must have a way to provide one venice.ai. Regulation can thus compel technical transparency solutions (like logging decision paths in smart contracts).
- **Open Standards and Interoperability:** Governments and international bodies can facilitate **standardization** for decentralized AI protocols. Similar to how internet protocols (TCP/IP, HTTP) were standardized through bodies like IETF and W3C, we might see AI network standards via organizations like IEEE or new coalitions. Regulators can adopt these standards in public procurement (e.g., requiring that AI systems purchased by government agencies use open, interoperable formats), spurring industry to follow. By doing so, they prevent vendor lock-in and ensure that, say, smart city AIs from different vendors can still share data or models – crucial for broad societal deployment.
- **Liability and Accountability Frameworks:** One of the thorniest issues: if a decentralized AI causes harm, how to assign liability? Regulators might consider novel approaches like **strict liability for certain AI outcomes** (like product liability: if an AI service causes damage, perhaps the developers of the algorithm are strictly liable, regardless of decentralization) or creating insurance schemes (maybe every AI network must carry insurance that pays out for damages, analogous to how car insurance works regardless of who's driving). In addition, there could be requirements for transparent governance in AI networks: for instance, if a DAO runs an AI service, maybe the DAO has to be a legal entity or have a representative who can be contacted. Some have proposed an idea

of **"legal personhood" for autonomous systems,** which could be controversial, but essentially treat a decentralized AI network as a corporate entity for legal purposes so it can sue or be sued. The EU parliament floated this idea in context of robotics but it's debated.

- **Ethical Guidelines and Oversight:** Many governments and organizations have issued AI ethical guidelines (avoid bias, ensure human oversight, etc.). Enforcing these in a decentralized context might involve requiring that any AI used in critical sectors (health, finance, transportation) has undergone audit by an independent body. That body could be a new kind of institution – perhaps an *Algorithmic Safety Board* – that certifies AI systems somewhat like how we certify medical devices or aircraft. They would look at the training data, the algorithm, outcomes from simulations, etc. Even if the AI is decentralized, the *protocols and models* could be audited. Regulation could mandate such audits and continuous monitoring. For bias, regulators could require that AI networks regularly test outcomes for disparate impact and have procedures to mitigate bias. Decentralization could actually help here – if models are local, you can test them in different communities for fairness and retrain locally to fix local biases.

- **Preventing Misuse and Ensuring Security:** There will likely be rules on what AI can be used for – e.g., bans or restrictions on autonomous weapons are being discussed internationally. Decentralized tech complicates enforcement (no central company to shut down), so regulators might focus on controlling inputs (like export controls on certain AI-enabling hardware, or penalties for individuals who deploy AI in prohibited ways). On security, regulators might impose requirements akin to cybersecurity frameworks: AI networks should follow certain encryption standards, consensus protocols must be robust (no known vulnerabilities), and perhaps even *red teaming* exercises mandated (like stress-tests for AI networks to see if they can withstand attacks). Governments themselves could participate in decentralized networks as *trust anchors* – for example, a government node that does nothing but validate that certain rules are being followed (like no personal data is leaking). If it finds an issue, it could alert or trigger a safe shutdown. This kind of regulatory node is a bit speculative but shows new roles regulators might take.

- **Empowering Consumers and Workers:** Laws might evolve to give individuals more rights regarding AI. For example, maybe a *"Right to Federate"* – meaning a user can demand that their data stays on their device and is used in a federated way rather than being uploaded. Or collective bargaining for workers could extend to algorithms – e.g., gig workers on a platform might demand a say in the algorithms assigning jobs (this could be facilitated by the platform switching to a decentralized governance where workers and clients have votes). Regulators can support this by legalizing and protecting algorithmic transparency rights and collective digital rights. Already, some jurisdictions consider requiring companies to consult workers when implementing significant AI systems that affect them (like scheduling algorithms).

One good thing: many policy makers are recognizing that involving multidisciplinary experts and the public in AI governance is important. We might see new **governance models** such as *regulatory sandboxes* for AI (where companies can try out decentralized AI solutions under regulator observation to gather data for sensible rules) and *participatory policy-making* (like citizen councils that discuss AI's local impacts). Decentralized AI's very ethos of distributed input could extend to regulation itself – maybe the networks will have built-in voting mechanisms where stakeholders, including end-users, can vote on updates or policies, and regulators might accept that as a form of compliance if certain broad principles are met.

International coordination will also be crucial. Decentralized networks don't respect borders; data flows globally. Bodies like the OECD, G20, or a specialized UN agency for AI (some propose something akin to an "International Atomic Energy Agency" but for AI) could harmonize rules or at least share best practices. If one region unilaterally bans or stifles some decentralized AI, it may just move elsewhere on the internet – so a collective approach is better.

In conclusion, governance and regulation have the challenging task of **guiding AI to align with societal values without strangling innovation**. For decentralized AI, regulators should focus on outcomes (safety, fairness, transparency) and foster open ecosystems rather than try to enforce centralized control (which is both antithetical to decentralization and likely impractical). They should also adapt legal concepts to new realities – possibly treating code or networks as actors in law, ensuring accountability is maintained even when there isn't a traditional corporate entity. Done right, regulation can *shape AI's future* to be one where its benefits are widely shared, risks are managed collaboratively, and public trust in AI allows its full potential to be realized for social good.

References:

1. SETI@home project description and history
    setiathome.berkeley.edu

    theatlantic.com

    en.wikipedia.org
2. Technical details of SETI@home's distributed computing model
    en.wikipedia.org

3. Impact and scale of SETI@home (volunteer computing power)
    en.wikipedia.org

4. BOINC and volunteer computing spin-offs
    en.wikipedia.org

5. Monolithic vs. decentralized AI definitions
    en.wikipedia.org

    provoke.fm

6. DeepSeek's architecture and efficiency innovations
   news.gsu.edu

7. DeepSeek's open-source and global reception
   weforum.org

   chaincatcher.com
8. Advantages of decentralized AI (distribution, resilience, data control)
   venice.ai

   provoke.fm
9. Challenges of decentralized AI (coordination, regulation)
   provoke.fm

   news.gsu.edu
10. Global brain concept and Internet as nervous system
    en.wikipedia.org

11. Goertzel's vision of a distributed blockchain-based AI network
    singularityhub.com

12. Neuroscience-inspired AI perspectives
    pubmed.ncbi.nlm.nih.gov

    numenta.com
13. Cognitive and biological parallels in deep learning and RL
    pubmed.ncbi.nlm.nih.gov

14. Venice.ai on decentralized AI and user control
    venice.ai

15. Decentralized AI applications in finance and healthcare
    provoke.fm

    pmc.ncbi.nlm.nih.gov

16. Ethical and legal considerations for AI (WEF and others)
    weforum.org

17. Importance of open, transparent development for positive AI outcomes
    singularityhub.com

www.ingramcontent.com/pod-product-compliance
Lightning Source LLC
LaVergne TN
LVHW052320060326
832902LV00023B/4517